Follow me III

Signage designs: defining spaces

SendPoints

Follow me III

Signage designs: defining spaces

SendPoints

EDITED & PUBLISHED BY SendPoints Publishing Co., Ltd.
PUBLISHER: Gengli Lin
PUBLISHING DIRECTOR: Shijian Lin
EDITORIAL DIRECTOR: Sundae Li
EXECUTIVE EDITOR: Luka Yu, Peiwei Zhou, Clytze Lee
ART DIRECTOR: Wanling He
EXECUTIVE ART EDITOR: Qiumei Lin
PROOFREADING: Sundae Li, Faith Dexter, Christina Hwang

ADDRESS: Room 15A Block 9 Tsui Chuk Garden, Wong Tai Sin, Kowloon, Hong Kong
TEL: +852-35832323 / **FAX:** +852-35832448
EMAIL: info@sendpoints.cn

DISTRIBUTED BY Guangzhou SendPoints Book Co., Ltd.
SALES MANAGER: Zhang Juan (China), Sissi (International)
GUANGZHOU: +86-20-89095121
BEIJING: +86-10-84139071
SHANGHAI: +86-21-63523469
EMAIL: overseas01@sendpoints.cn
WEBSITE: www.sendpoints.cn

ISBN 978-988-13834-1-9

Printed and bound in China

FOREWORD

By Sarah Manning & Peter Feldmann, Space Agency, London

At its most essential, signage design is directly concerned with fundamental human needs, such as being able to travel effectively, to find one's way back home, to let others know where one can be found, or get away safely from a dangerous situation.

Buildings and cities can, but unfortunately in many cases do not, provide the necessary signals that facilitate intuitive orientation. City grids are not always straight or complete, ways in and out are not always visible, landmarks cannot be relied upon from every perspective. To assist people in finding their way, signage is often added as an afterthought to the design of environments.

'Wayfinding' refers to the contemporary field devoted to planning and designing coherent systems which incorporate maps, signs, directional markers and the insertion of small clues throughout the built environment that enable orientation in cultural and geographic landscapes. Good wayfinding systems employ explicit signs and information as well as implicit cues and symbols.

The process of constructing a "mental map" requires both perceptual information acquired directly through the senses, and inferences about things that cannot directly be seen but which add to the intelligibility of the space one is in. For those with a strong spatial orientation, a mental map may consist of an overview of the space, oriented to the compass. For these people, an overarching framework has been constructed, into which the smaller pieces of information can fit. For those whose style of navigation is based more on their own eye-level perspective, a path needs to hold a series of cues at each important decision point. Their path can be retraced through the memory of certain markers along the way.

The role of the wayfinding designer is to uncover the latent structure of a building or urban space and to make it visible to first-time visitors. The wayfinding system codes the environment - through naming systems which identify, through colour which differentiates, through numbering systems which perceptually order the space, by the imposition of hierarchies which cast greater importance on some places rather than others. In so doing, the designer not only reveals the hidden logic of the place, but also influences the perception and use of space.

What the more contemporary wayfinding projects share is a philosophy of seamlessness, in which the way is not just shown by text-based signage, but also by techniques which unify a layer of graphic communication with the fabric of the architecture and landscape. Trading in an additive approach for an integrated approach, these projects treat wayfinding as a holistic part of the design using perceptual cues made from directional lighting, colour, materials, embedded markers, supergraphics and iconography. Strong wayfinding systems provide a coherent, unified voice within an environment.

Viewing signage as an integral point of communication between people and their environments, the wayfinding system mediates between architecture and human perception. By acting as the user interface in the built environment, it adds another, more familiar language to the architecture - one of words, colour, illustration, shape. The use of visual narrative imbues places with identity as well as orientation.

It is this mediated layer of information, which is growing in importance within our contemporary world. Increasingly, we rely on mediated information at our fingertips to augment our experience and our procession through different environments. However, as humans, we still seek real experiences which engage the senses, and not only digital ones. In this context, wayfinding systems must seamlessly integrate real space, information and mobile/wearable technology into a single experience. Wayfinding design is part of the informational layer through which we navigate the world.

The selection of contemporary signage designs displayed here, not only address the basic human needs for orientation; but transcend this role, and elevate the discipline to one which shapes people's experience and inspires the imagination.

LEISURE SPACE

EDUCATIONAL AND MEDICAL INSTITUTIONS

Wayfinding in Educational and Medical institutions: The Emotional Appeal

In school buildings, wayfinding designers try their best to avoid boring and lifeless directional prompts. Most designs in these places are bold, oversized and experimental. They rely on visual exhibitions and employ innovative concepts that impart energy. They strive not to simply lead students to the right places, but also activate their emotions. The signage system in educational institutions is a form of encouragement and inspiration to students. Sign should never bore students even though they turn up in the same spot every day.

The function of emotional appeal is also taken seriously in wayfinding design for medical institutions such as hospitals. The lingering depressing and unnerving atmosphere needs to be effectively mitigated. Consequently, wayfinding graphics in hospitals are usually colorful and animated, enlivening the plain white walls, infusing the patients with renewed energy. In this case, signage is no longer merely a clear guidance to patients. To people who have fears or concerns, it acts like a companion, constantly giving them spiritual support.

In both educational and medical institutions, the emotional appeal expressed by wayfinding language is highly valued. It influences users and caters to the distinct personality of the institution, advocating its core value.

Find & Discover

The signage system for Design, Architecture & Building Faculty reflects views of contemporary technology and development.

Red and yellow routes are painted on the ground. These veins go through laboratories and workshop to form a planform resembling a circuit diagram, giving off a sense of technological advancement. The signage stretches throughout the faculty, encouraging students to follow and arrive at the right laboratory where further exploration can be conducted.

Design Firm: BrandCulture Communications Pty Ltd **Designer:** Antonijo Bacic, Terry Curtis **Photographer:** Studio Commercial **Client:** University of Technology Sydney **Location:** Sydney, Australia

Student
2500

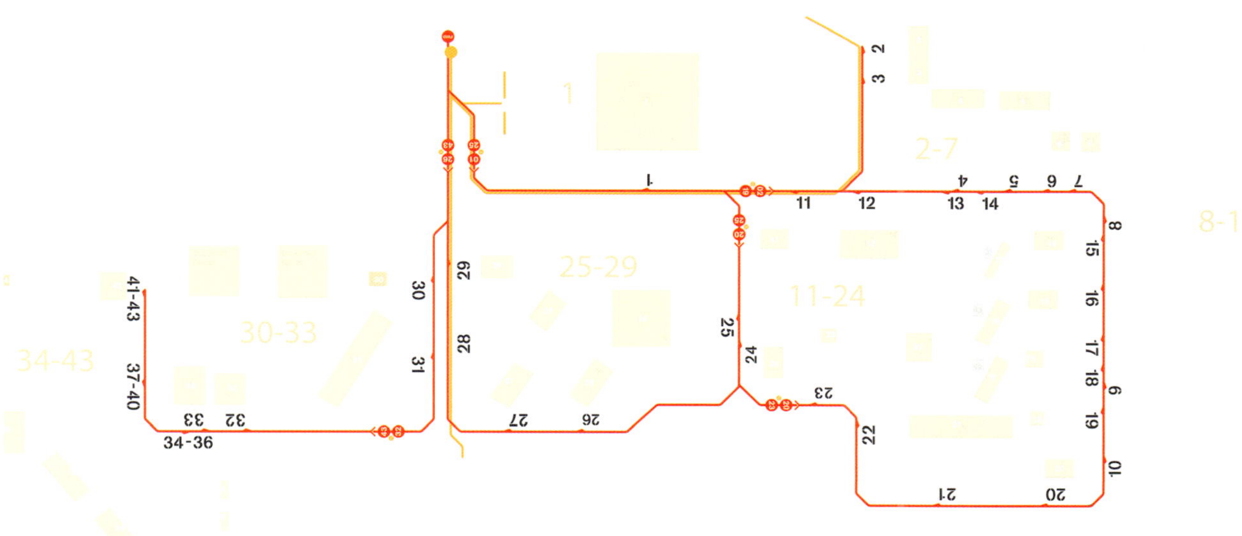
1
2-7
25-29
11-24
30-33
34-43
34-36
37-40
41-43

CLEMCO
17

TO
19

FIND

01
25
26
TO
43

Lucerne University

An old post distribution centre was refurbished as the new building of Lucerne University. The signage blends in with the walls; on the lower levels huge numbers are shown on white and silver concrete walls while on the upper levels numbers are embedded in green and purple plaster. Further wayfinding information is placed on boards with flexible frames. The floor numbers are arresting and synchronize with the interior decoration.

Design Firm: Hi **Designer:** Megi Zumstein ,Claudio Barandun **Photographer:** Roger Frei, Mitch Enzmann, Hi **Client:** Canton of Lucerne **Location:** Lucerne, Switzerland

UNI
PH

HÖRSAAL 1

B
A

A
3.A01 — 3.A19
3.A18 — 3.A52
B
3.B01 — 3.B44
3.B45 — 3.B58

B
A

B
2.B01 – 2.B23
A
2.A01 – 2.A46
UNIVERSITÄT
PÄDAGOGISCHE HOCHSCHULE
ZENTRAL- UND HOCHSCHULBIBLIOTHEK
HÖRSÄLE 1–8 / MENSA
HÖRSÄLE 9/10/11

ZENTRAL- UND
HOCHSCHUL
BIBLIOTHEK

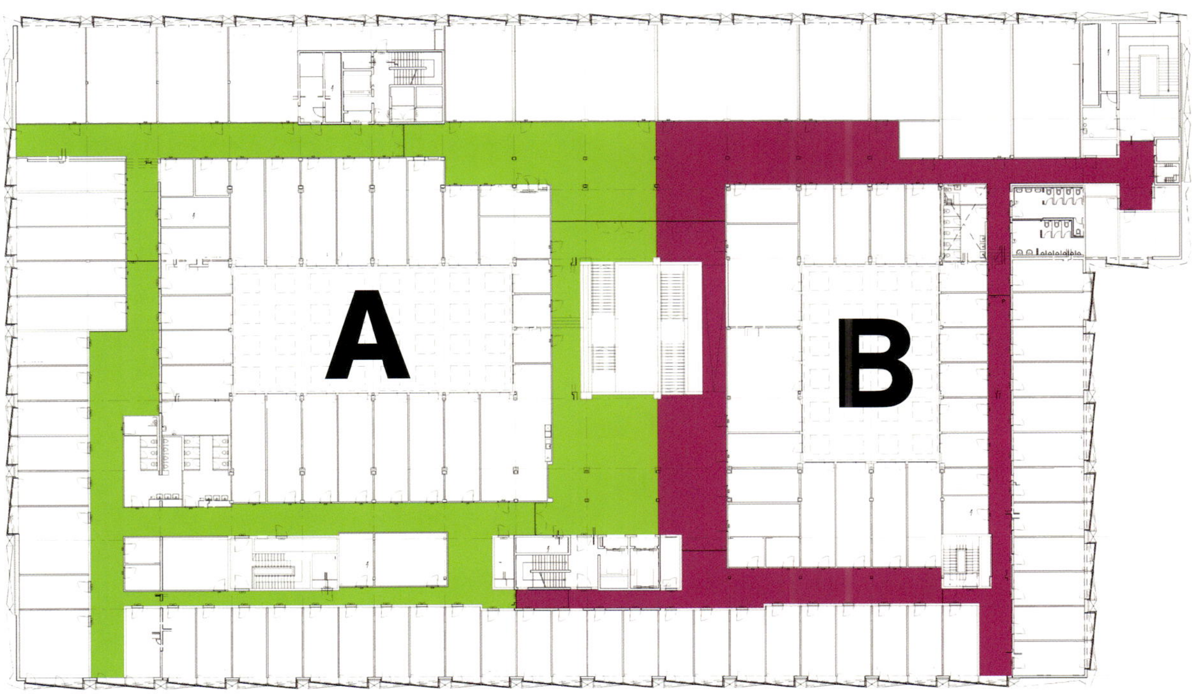
A
B

Quinta das Flores High School

The designers focused on this music school's special tie with sound waves and created a customized typeface and a series of pictograms comprised of vertical black strips which visualize sound waves. The idea of sound intensity is translated into the design by differentiating the density of strips in the typeface according to the numerical value of the floor; the higher the floor is, the bolder the strips are. A compact arrangement of alternating space and strips symbolizes sound intermingled with silence. The oversized typeface suits the large and open architecture. The signage was stenciled directly onto the concrete walls in an inexpensive way. This ingenious and effective system visually interacts with sounds and shows off key features of the music school.

Design Firm: R2 **Art & Creative Direction:** Lizá Ramalho and Artur Rebelo **Design:** Lizá Ramalho and Artur Rebelo, assisted by Sébastien Fisher and Maria de Sousa **Photographer:** Nélson Garrido **Client:** Parque Escolar E.P.E. **Location:** Coimbra, Portugal

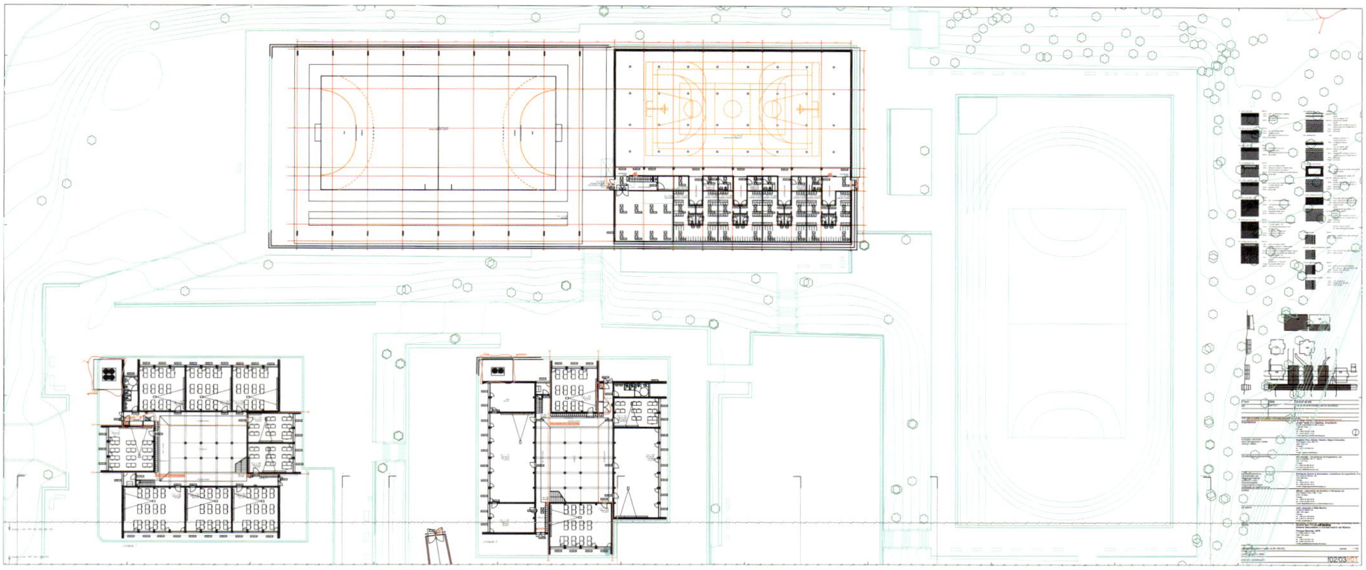

ADMINISTRATIVO P
AUDITÓRIO
CANTINA / BAR
WC
BIBLIOTECA

R1/50
R1/41
R1/42
R1/43
R1/44
R1/45
R1/46
R1/47
R1/48
R1/49

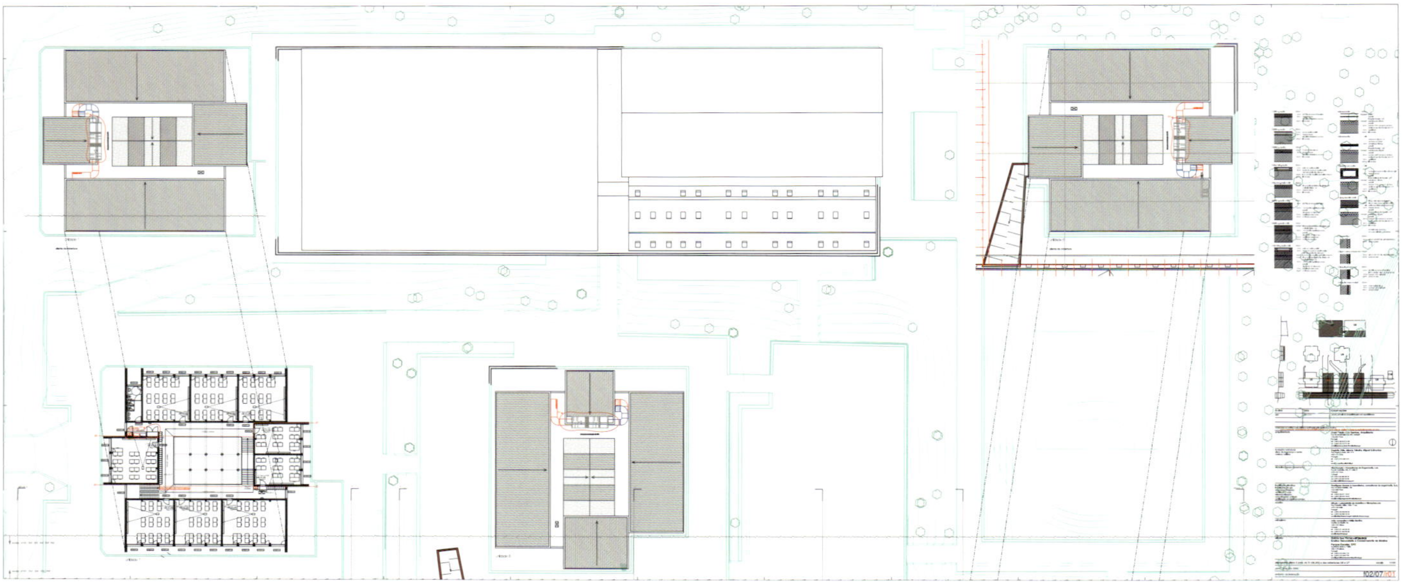

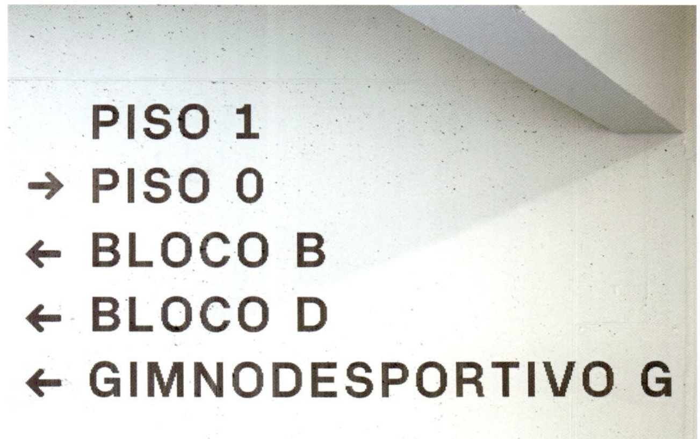
PISO 1
→ PISO 0
← BLOCO B
← BLOCO D
← GIMNODESPORTIVO G

BAR

ESCOLA SECUNDÁRIA 3CEB QUINTA DAS FLORES
CONSERVATÓRIO DE MÚSICA DE COIMBRA

Faculty of Graphic Design

The designer uses inconsistency as an element in the signage project for this old faculty building in Academy of Fine Arts in Gdansk. Different typefaces flow together, assembling information and graphics in fluctuating sizes on the wall. The signage offers students unambiguous guidance. It also complements and emphasizes the diversity, creativity and timeless design principles of the faculty.

Designer: Julia Parchimowicz **Client:** Polis Litoral Sudoeste **Location:** Gdansk, Poland

6
5
4
3
2
1
W

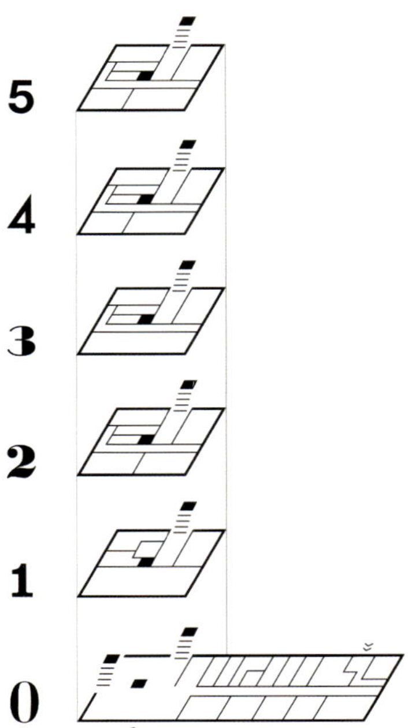
5
4
3
2
1
0

204 P
Pracownia Podstaw
Komunikacji Wizualnej
204 P
Pracownia Podstaw
Komunikacji Wizualnej
W
winda
W
winda
104
204
12
407
10
306
406
13
T
G
R
S
D
E
O

The Innovation Center

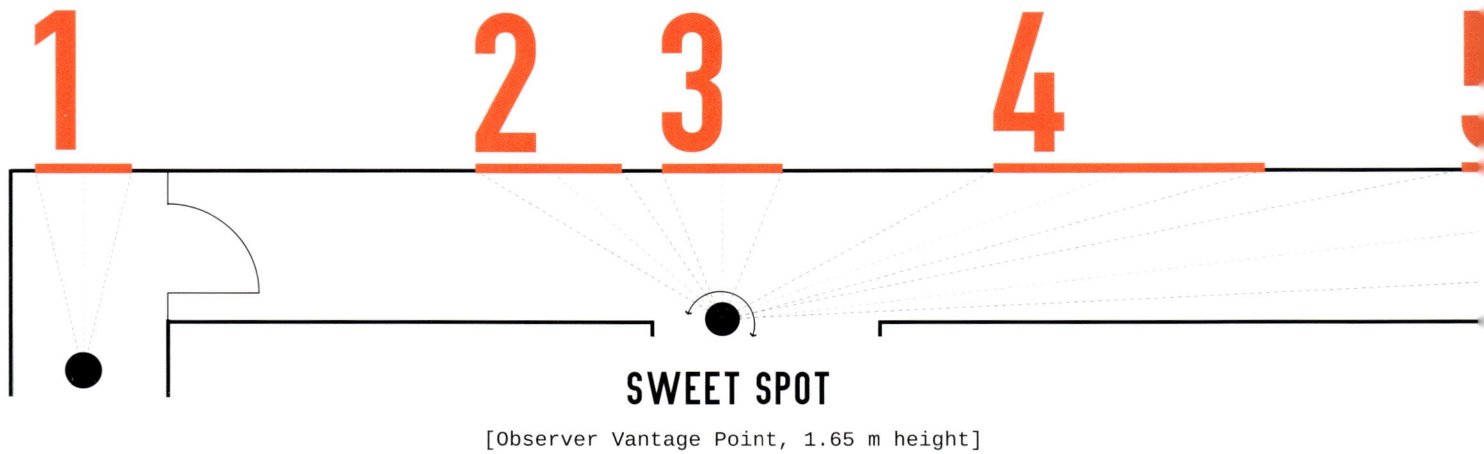

Design Firm: Claan / Clara Vieira, Andreas Eberharter **Designer:** Clara Vieira, Andreas Eberharter **Photographer:** Claan

Client: Science and Technology Park of University of Porto **Location:** Porto, Portugal

The designer tailored a signage system expanding beyond the walls to turn the innovation center into a landmark. The initial bland corridors are filled with colors and vitality through the visually invasive graphics interspersed across the space and the creation of illusion. As visitors step into the intersection of the entrance hall and corridors, numbers of laboratories on the same wall are perceived in perfect shape and size from the visual "sweet spot". As visitors leave their position to approach a laboratory entrance, the numbers become bigger and bigger until a final point of total distortion. By using anamorphic typography the design establishes a connection between simple numbers and scientific measurement; it challenges the conventional idea that innovation can only be realized through technological advancement. The signage system is bold and dynamic, adding playfulness and joy to the hall's walls. Besides identifying laboratories and leading the visitors, the bright, luminous, red color represents prohibition and creates a natural hesitation before knocking or stepping into the sterile research facilities. With this modern and experimental signage design, an environment conductive to innovation is brought about.

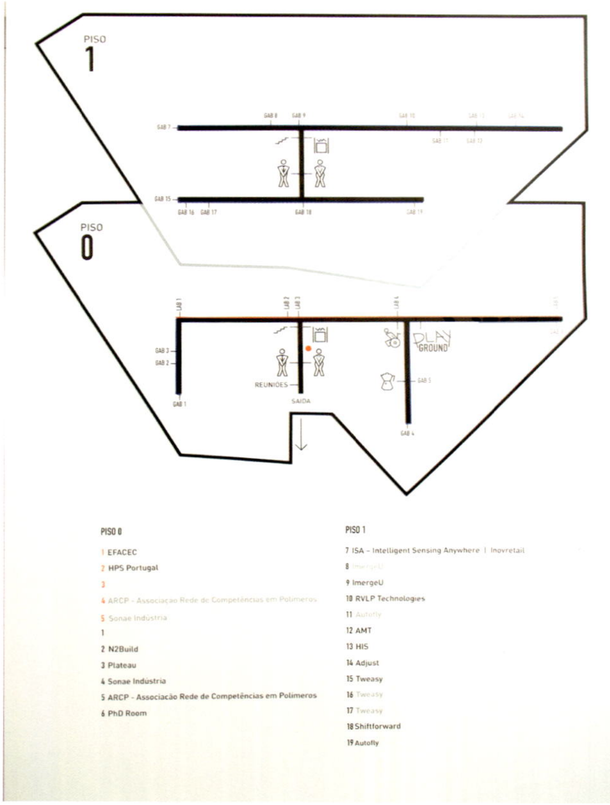
PISO 1
PISO 0
PLAY GROUND
SAIDA
PISO 0
1 EFACEC
2 HPS Portugal
3
4 ARCP - Associaçao Rede de Competências em Polimeros
5 Sonae Indústria
1
2 N2Build
3 Plateau
4 Sonae Indústria
5 ARCP - Associacão Rede de Competências em Polimeros
6 PhD Room
PISO 1
7 ISA – Intelligent Sensing Anywhere | Inovretail
8
9 ImergeU
10 RVLP Technologies
11 Autofly
12 AMT
13 HIS
14 Adjust
15 Tweasy
16 Tweasy
17 Tweasy
18 Shiftforward
19 Autofly

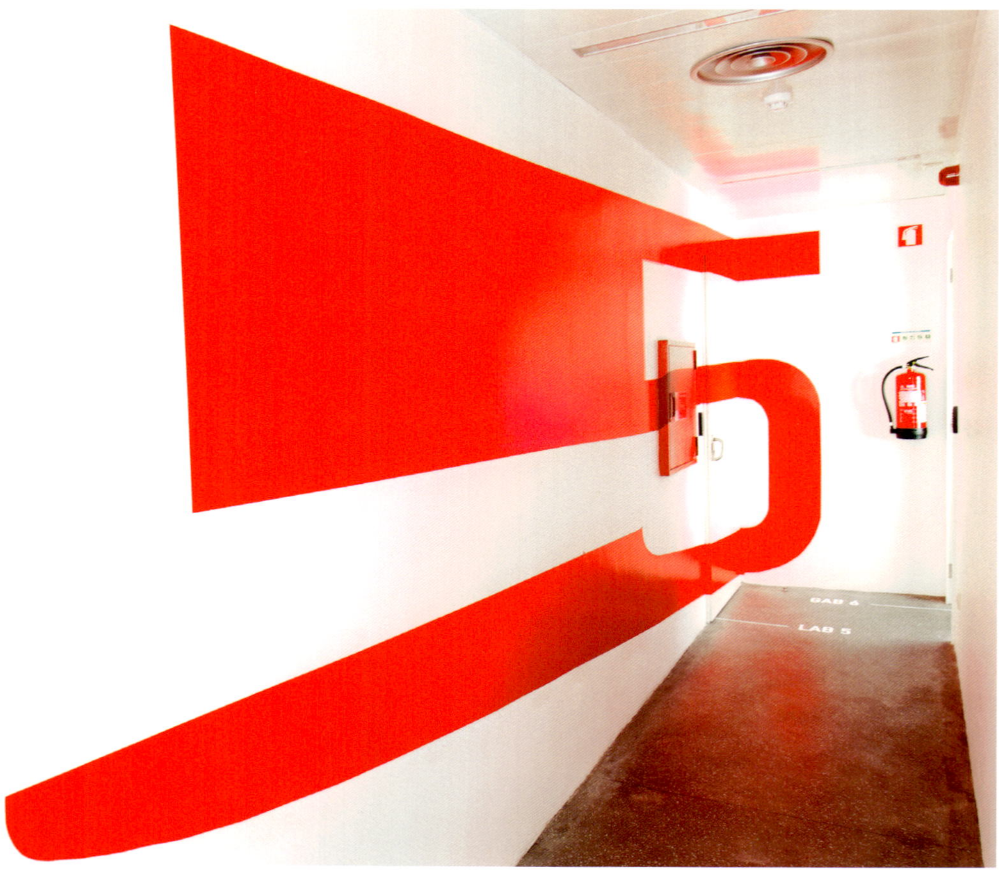
GAB 4
LAB 5

PISO
0

PLAY
GROUND

NCPA Campus Signage Design

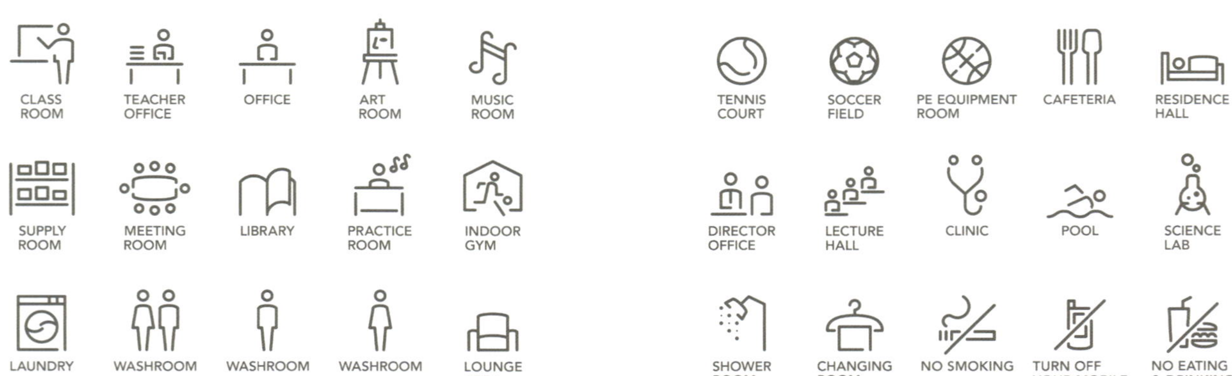

Design Firm: The Box Brand Design Co., Ltd **Designer:** Joey Lo, Edmond Li,Terry Lai, Yvonne Chung **Photographer:** Joey Lo **Client:** International Schools Services **Location:** Nansha, China

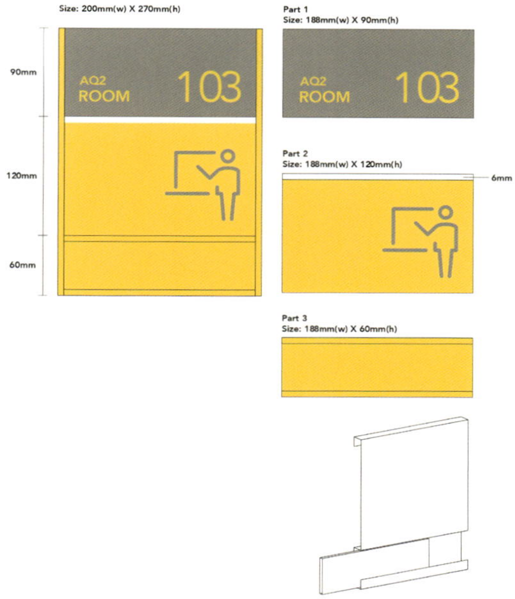

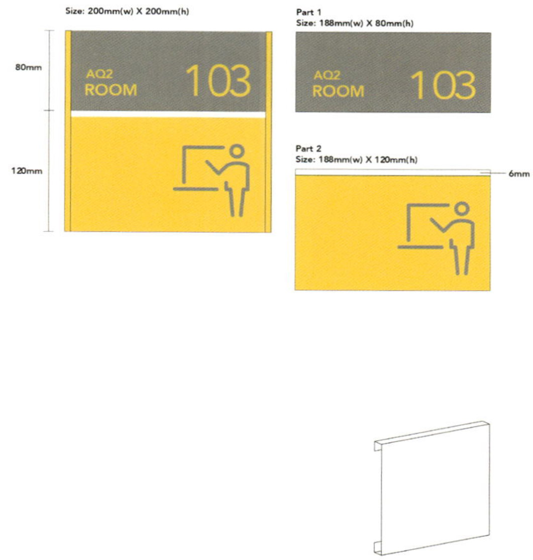

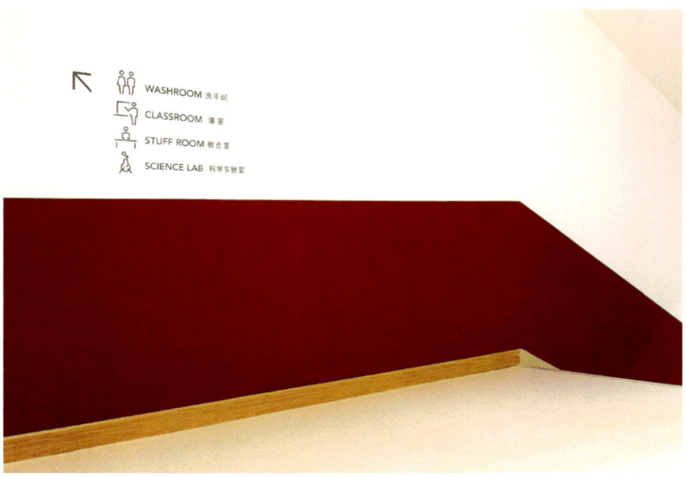

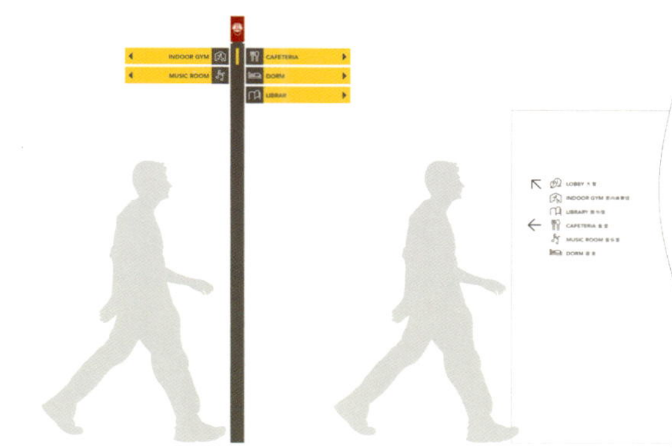

As the first American high school in Southern China, NCPA has a modern campus. To match their image and campus environment, a series of interesting and stylish pictograms were created. Unlike traditional campus signs in China, each signage in NCPA campus represents different departments with creative graphics. The bright, sunny colors used in guidance evoke a feeling of youth and vigor. This wayfinding system spreads the innovative ideas of a modern high school.

Deakin University Library

To create a cohesive look for the signage system, the designer borrowed the rotated D-shape emblem of Deakin University. The basic D-shape is consistently applied throughout the design. Three levels are divided by three main color groups, and each section of the library has its own color. Three forms of library maps are implemented: main signboard, wall printing, and pocket maps. The fresh and evident color coding of levels and sections as well as the well-placed maps make navigation of the library intuitive and effortless. This Wayfinding design proposal complements the library interior by its shape, curve and colour.

Design Firm: Kine Halland **Designer:** Kine Halland **Photographer:** Kine Halland **Client:** Deakin University **Location:** Melbourne, Australia

NO EXIT
NO EXIT
DEAKIN
Worldly

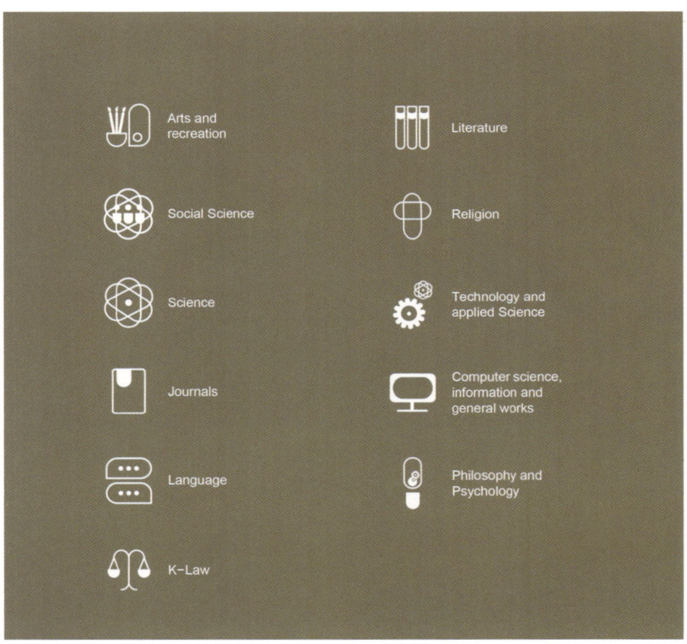
Arts and recreation
Literature
Social Science
Religion
Science
Technology and applied Science
Journals
Computer science, information and general works
Language
Philosophy and Psychology
K-Law

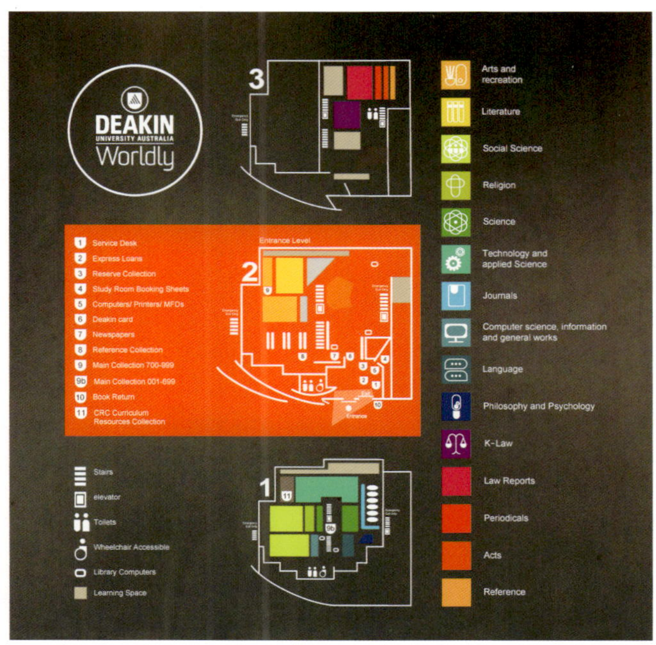
DEAKIN
UNIVERSITY AUSTRALIA
Worldly
3
Entrance Level
2
1 Service Desk
2 Express Loans
3 Reserve Collection
4 Study Room Booking Sheets
5 Computers/ Printers/ MFDs
6 Deakin card
7 Newspapers
8 Reference Collection
9 Main Collection 700-999
9a Main Collection 001-699
10 Book Return
11 CRC Curriculum Resources Collection
Entrance
1
Stairs
elevator
Toilets
Wheelchair Accessible
Library Computers
Learning Space
Arts and recreation
Literature
Social Science
Religion
Science
Technology and applied Science
Journals
Computer science, information and general works
Language
Philosophy and Psychology
K-Law
Law Reports
Periodicals
Acts
Reference

2
Express
Loans
1
Service
Desk
2
LEVEL
DEAKIN
Worldly

10
Book
Return

Language
Science

Building 2, Institute of Electrical Engineering, Stuttgart University

The previous signage system weakly contrasted with the silver-coloured background was redesigned. With particular emphasis on color contrast, the black lettering is now clearly printed on fluorescent-coloured backgrounds. The poignant and effective contrast makes for an eye-catching result: the messages stand out in neon shades against the grey concrete walls, proclaiming: READ THIS! Resembling test paper, the signage remains consistent with an institute of science.

Design Firm: büro uebele visuelle kommunikation **Designer:** Katharina Moritzen, Felix Rabe, Katrin Theile, Andreas Uebele **Photographer:** Daniel Fels
Client: Universitätsbauamt Stuttgart und Hohenheim **Location:** Stuttgart, Germany

Fachbereich Elektrotechnik und Informationstechnik

Ebene U1
0
1
2
Institut für Energieübertragung und Hochspannungstechnik
Institut für Halbleitertechnik ←
Institut für Elektrische Energiewandlung →

INTO University of East Anglia Center

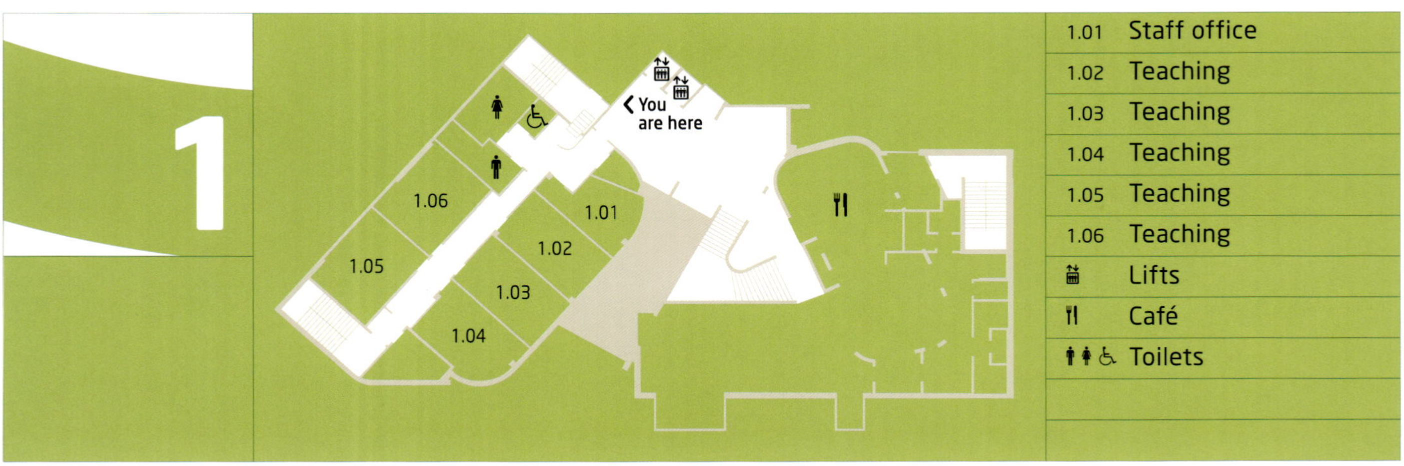

Isolated segments of INTO'S round secondary logo are combined with fresh colors to visually distinguish levels. Large, clear floor information uses these irregular and relaxing segments as backgrounds. The signage system works in harmony with the dynamic nature of a center for international students, providing a pervasive academic environment.

Design Firm: Richard Wise **Designer:** Andy Uren, Richard Wise **Photographer:** Signbox and INTO University Partnerships **Client:** INTO University of East Anglia **Location:** Norwich, UK

FIND YOUR WAY
0

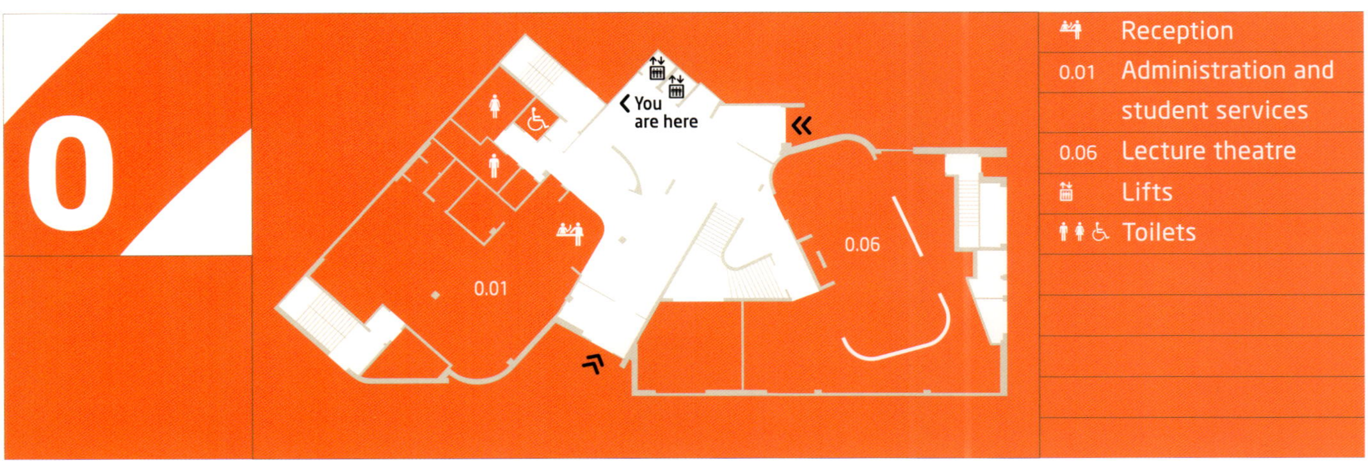
0
You are here
0.01
0.06
Reception
0.01 Administration and student services
0.06 Lecture theatre
Lifts
Toilets

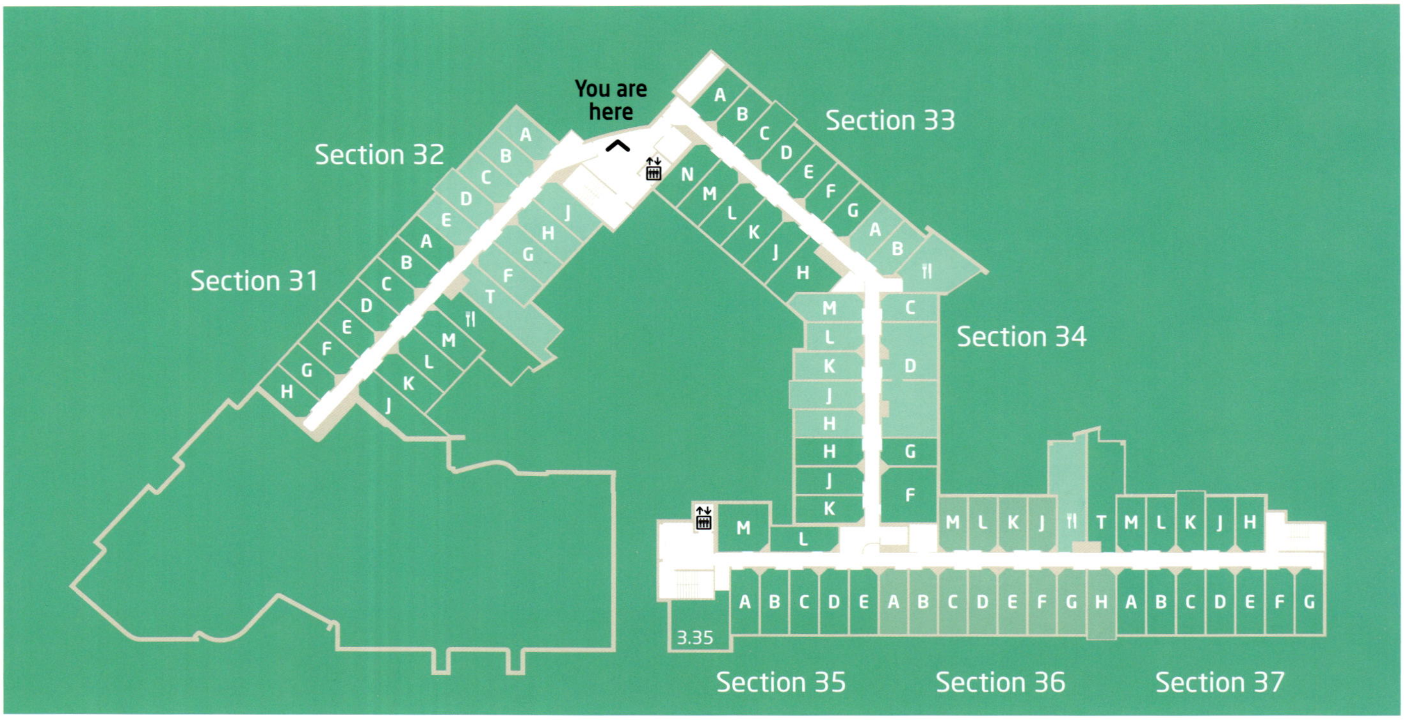
You are here
Section 31
Section 32
Section 33
Section 34
Section 35
Section 36
Section 37
3.35

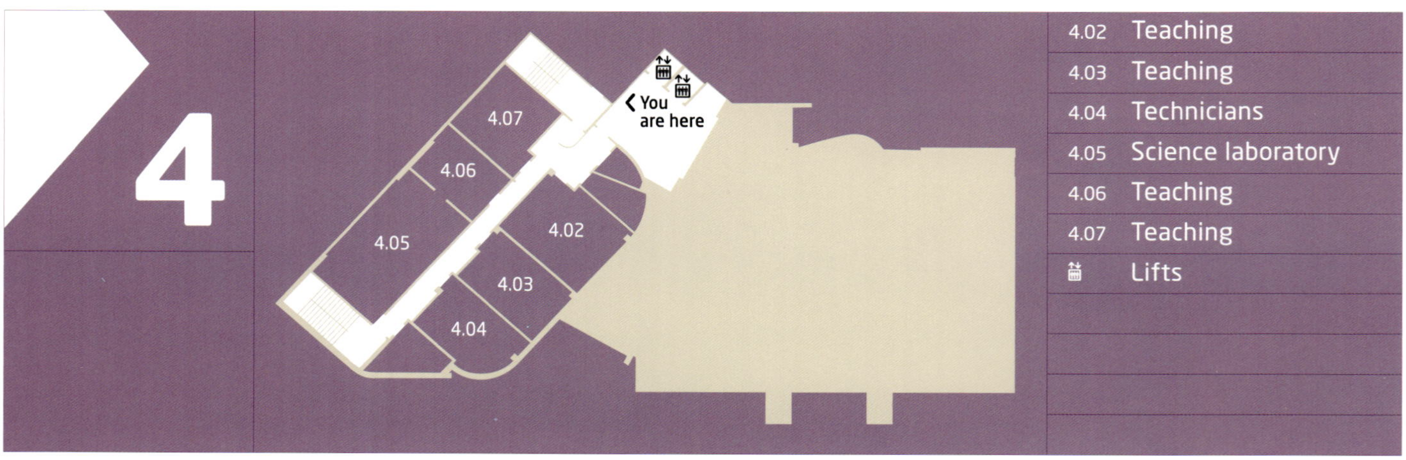
4
You are here
4.02
4.03
4.04
4.05
4.06
4.07
4.02 Teaching
4.03 Teaching
4.04 Technicians
4.05 Science laboratory
4.06 Teaching
4.07 Teaching
Lifts

2

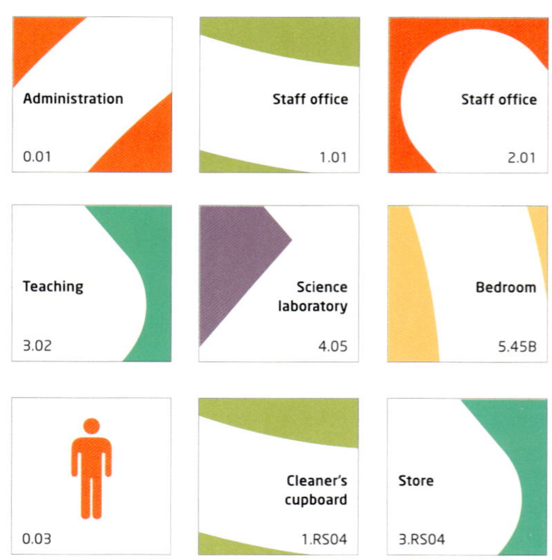
Administration
0.01
Staff office
1.01
Staff office
2.01
Teaching
3.02
Science laboratory
4.05
Bedroom
5.45B
0.03
Cleaner's cupboard
1.RS04
Store
3.RS04

FIND YOUR WAY:
0

CAFÉ
1

0
2
3
4
5
1

4

Saldus Music and Art School

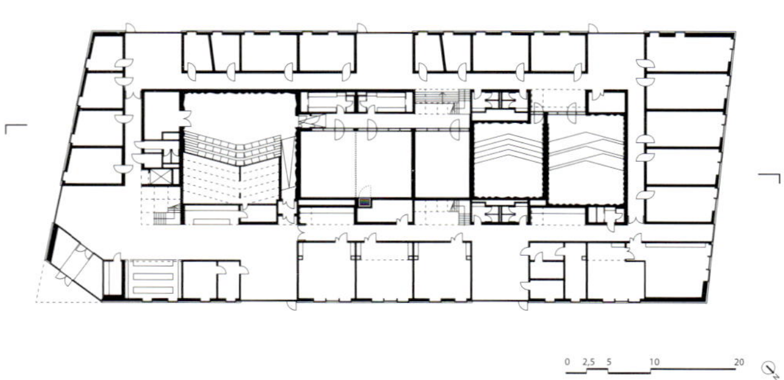

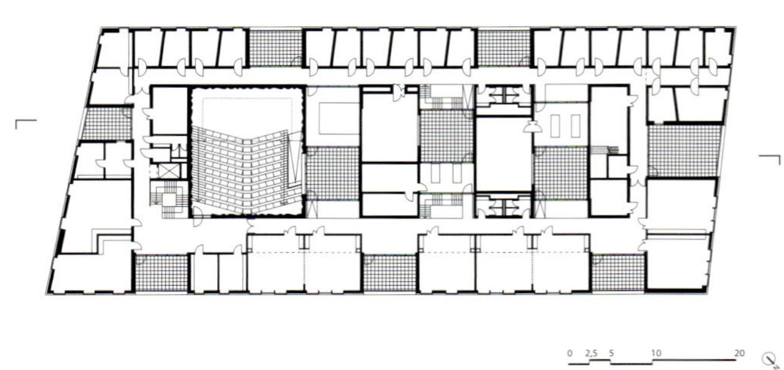

This building comprises two separate schools. Color distinction is applied to visually distinguish the two institutions. Green denotes the music school while blue stands for the art school. Signage and pictograms in white and clean lines are presented on colorful backgrounds. Comfortable and refreshing surroundings are created through natural interior design and the accompanying simple signage system.

Designer: Mikelis Putrams, Linda Krumina **Photographer:** Ansis Starks **Client:** Regional Municipality of Saldus **Location:** Saldus, Latvia

2
23

2
01

Martin Luther King School

Since children spend such long hours at school, the interior and exterior signage system in this school is particularly designed for children. The mandate for the wayfinding was to find a creative and educational solution that could not only guide but also engage and appeal to children. This is why the environmental design operation was conceived in child-like language: respectful, funny and educational. The common spaces, walls, and corridors become communication vehicles, with signs which could communicate messages in comic, contemporary language. Children can learn to read and count while exploring these nooks and crannies. These child-oriented designed elements link to the total signage system of the school, encouraging children to delve into their curiosity, their school, and the world.

Design Firm: ma:design **Designer:** Massimiliano Patrignani, Monica Zaffini **Photographer:** StudioLux **Client:** Municipality of Maiolati Spontini **Location:** Ancona, Italy

LA BA—LE—NA NON È BA—NA—LE!
PRESERVA
RISPETTA
PROTEGGI
AMA

26

LO DICE LA LEGGE
CI SONO TUTTI I MIEI AMICI
POSSO GIOCARE A CALCIO IN PALESTRA
VADO A
I go to school becaus

Dauro Oliveira Orthodontics Clinic

The concept of the signage project for Dauro Oliveira Orthodontics Clinic stemmed from brackets and rubber bands. Pictograms and numbers were created, drawn by material inspired by the above elements used in orthodontics treatment.

The signage encourages interactions between the patients and the environment while sharing the idea that at the end of the often painful path lies a brighter smile.

Design Firm: Greco Design **Designer:** Gustavo Greco, Tidé, Fred Fita, Victor Fernandes, Alexandre Fonseca, Dani Pires **Photographer:** Victor Magalhães
Client: Dauro Oliveira **Location:** Belo Horizonte, Brazil

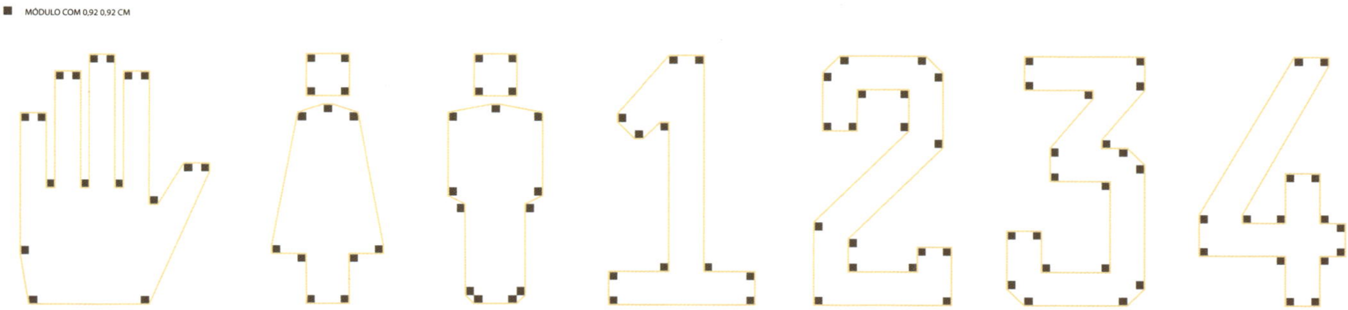
MÓDULO COM 0,92 0,92 CM

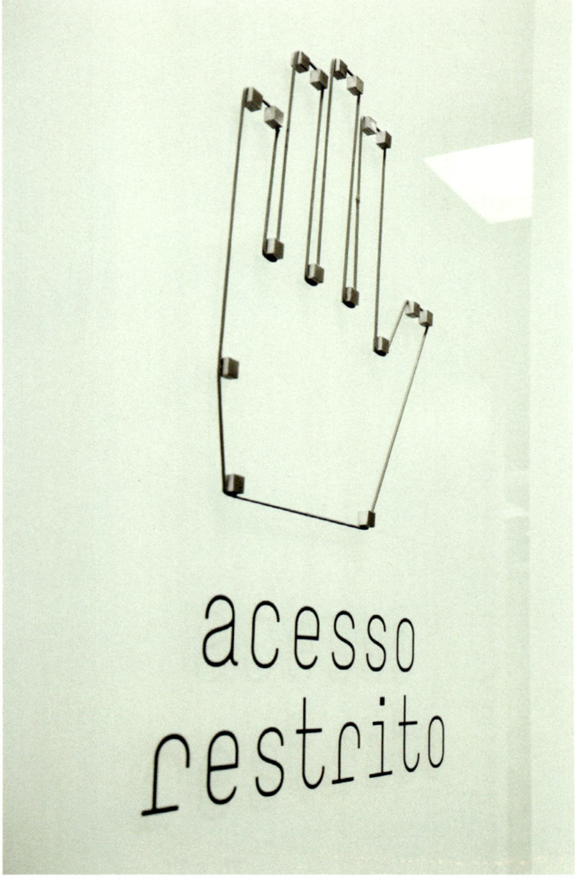
acesso
restrito

Kawagoe Red Cross Blood Donation Room

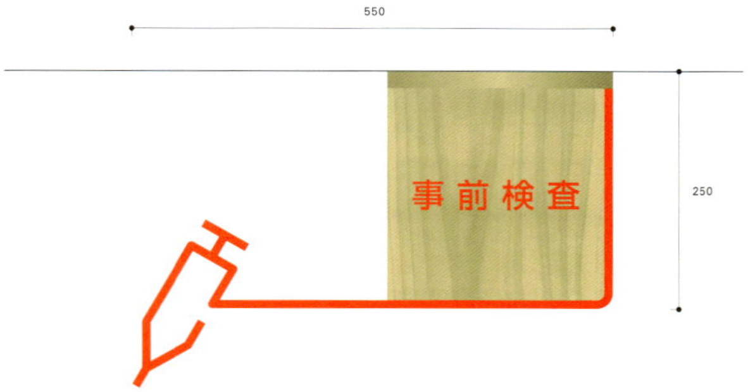

カウンター卓上サイン　事前検査カウンター

突き出しサイン　ドリンク

Design Firm: 6D **Designer:** Shogo Kishino, Nozomi Tagami **Photographer:** 6D **Client:** Japanese Red Cross Society **Location:** Kawagoe, Japan

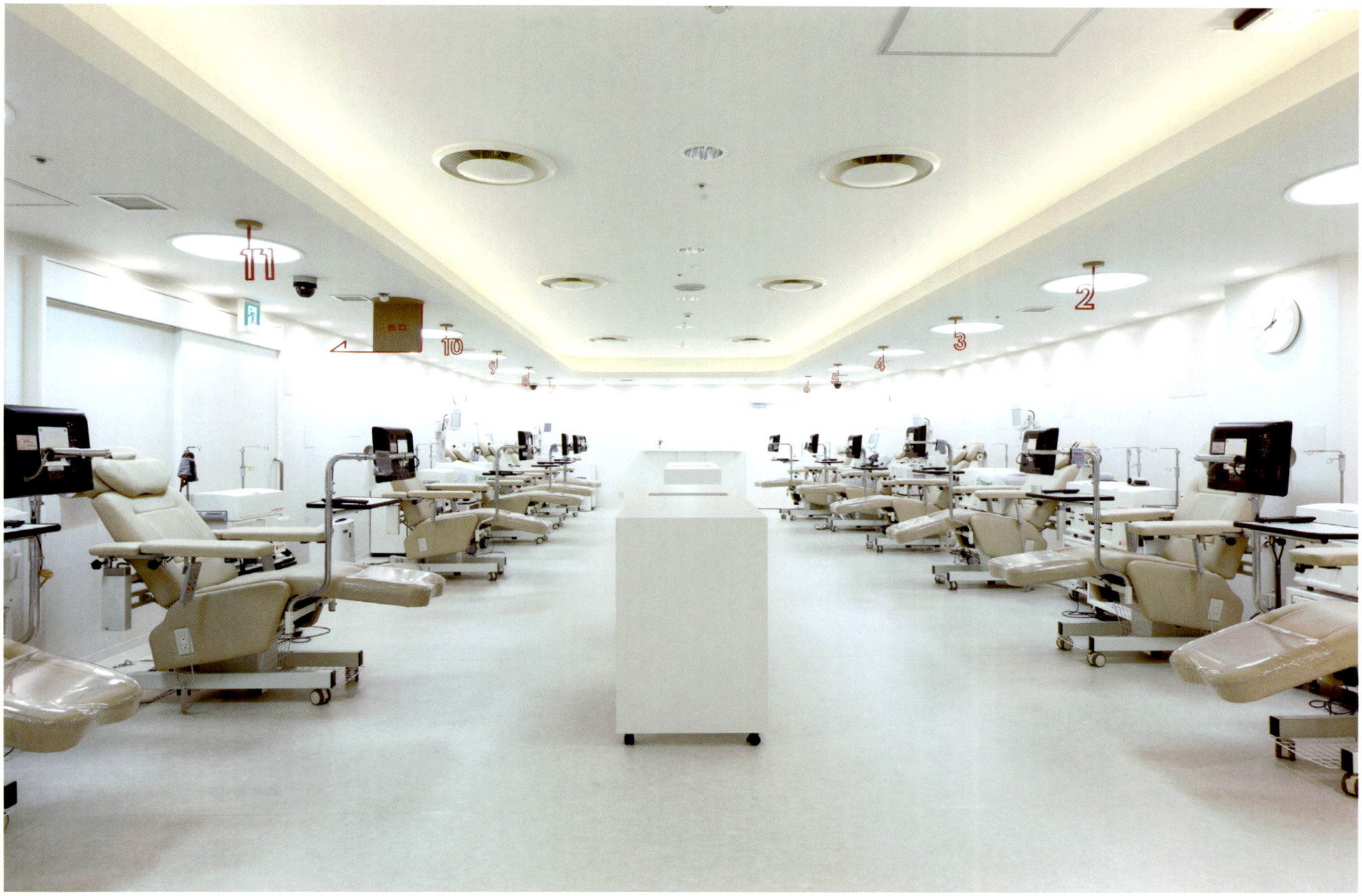

吊りサイン　出口

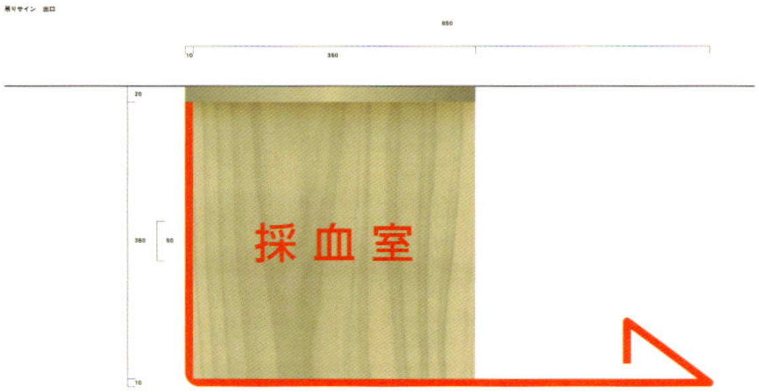

使用フォント
日本語：A-OTF新ゴPro M
英語：Swiss721 BT Medium

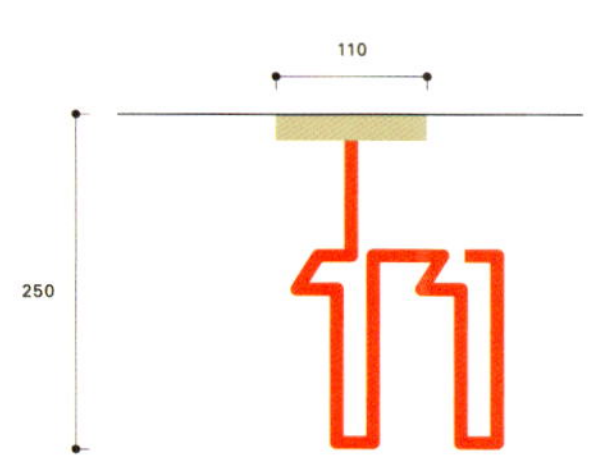

吊りサイン　ベッド番号

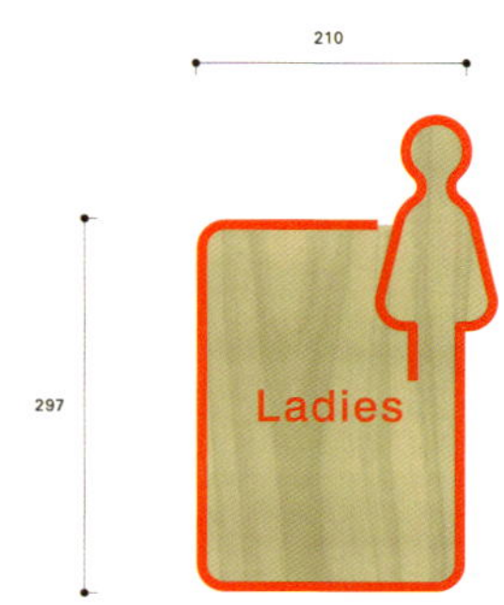

壁付サイン　問診室 1・2

1

2

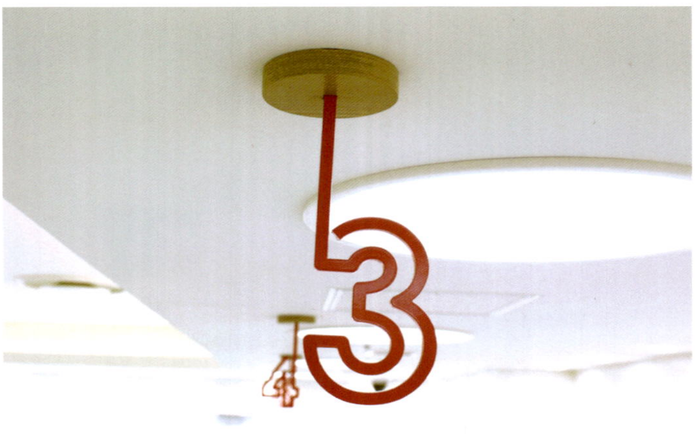
3

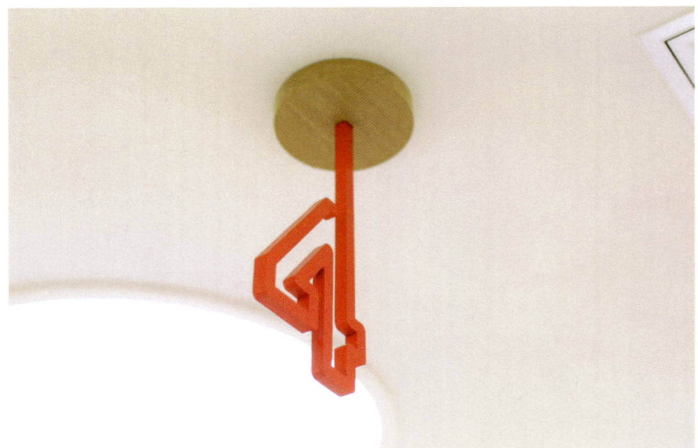
4

問診室
1

問診室
2

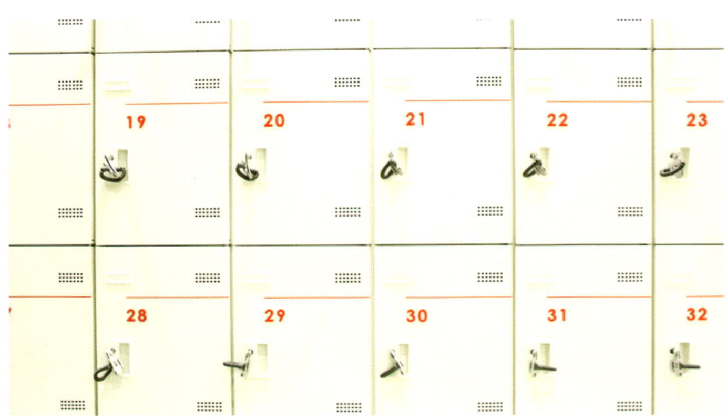
19
20
21
22
23
28
29
30
31
32

In the blood donation room, numbers hang from the ceiling in a red, outlined font to guide volunteers to the appropriate beds; all of the pictograms are invented with simple strokes. The junctions of the signage and the ceilings or walls are wooden roundels, creating a delicate and soothing visual impact. The modern tridimensional signage system jumps into visitors' view and is plainly recognized. The red lines in wayfinding are relaxing to people, also echoing the selfless blood circulation in the world.

Doctor & Co

The main objective of the signage design for this medical clinic is to functionally navigate while removing patients' psychological barriers towards visiting doctors. The oversized pictograms convey a light-hearted mood. Because the wayfinding information is embedded into relaxing environmental graphics, this signage design eliminates tension and contributes to a greater confidence from the patients.

Design Firm: Mountteam **Designer:** Tigran Kazaryan **Photographer:** Ivan Petrov **Client:** Government of Moscow **Location:** Moscow, Russia

Попробуйте проверить
свое зрение до того
как зашли в кабинет
Если вы смогли
дойти до этих строк
то у вас хорошее зрение
11
Офтальмолог
10
пожарный
выход

Women
Men

Во время мануальной терапии
мышцы тела необходимо
держать в полностью
расслабленном состоянии

Embryo Clinic

Aiming at distinguishing this new medical facility from its competitors, the team designed an elegant and friendly brand identity. The color palette of green and blue hues is inviting and professional, injecting drops of colors and lightsome mood into the signage system. The identity is seamlessly integrated into the clinic's architecture and wayfinding system, substituting brand elements with playful solutions, and therefore maintaining a fluid visual consistency.

Design Firm: MALVI **Designer:** Panos Voulgaris, Maria Malindretou-Vika **Photographer:** Giorgio Papadopoulos **Client:** Embryo Clinic **Location:** Greece

1
2

A
ΓΡΑΦΕΙΟ
CONSULTING

Υποδοχή
Reception

Surya Child Care

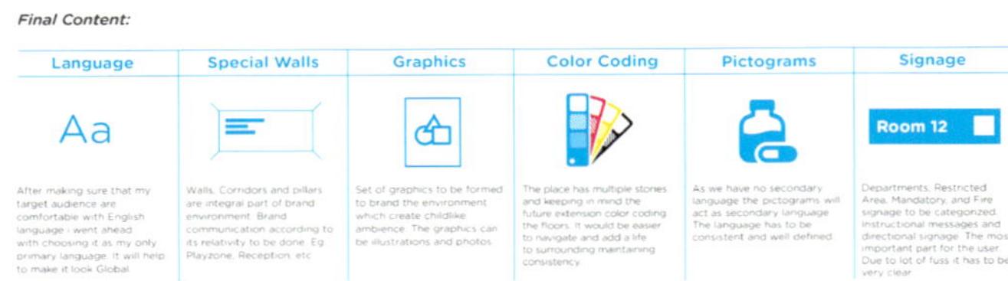

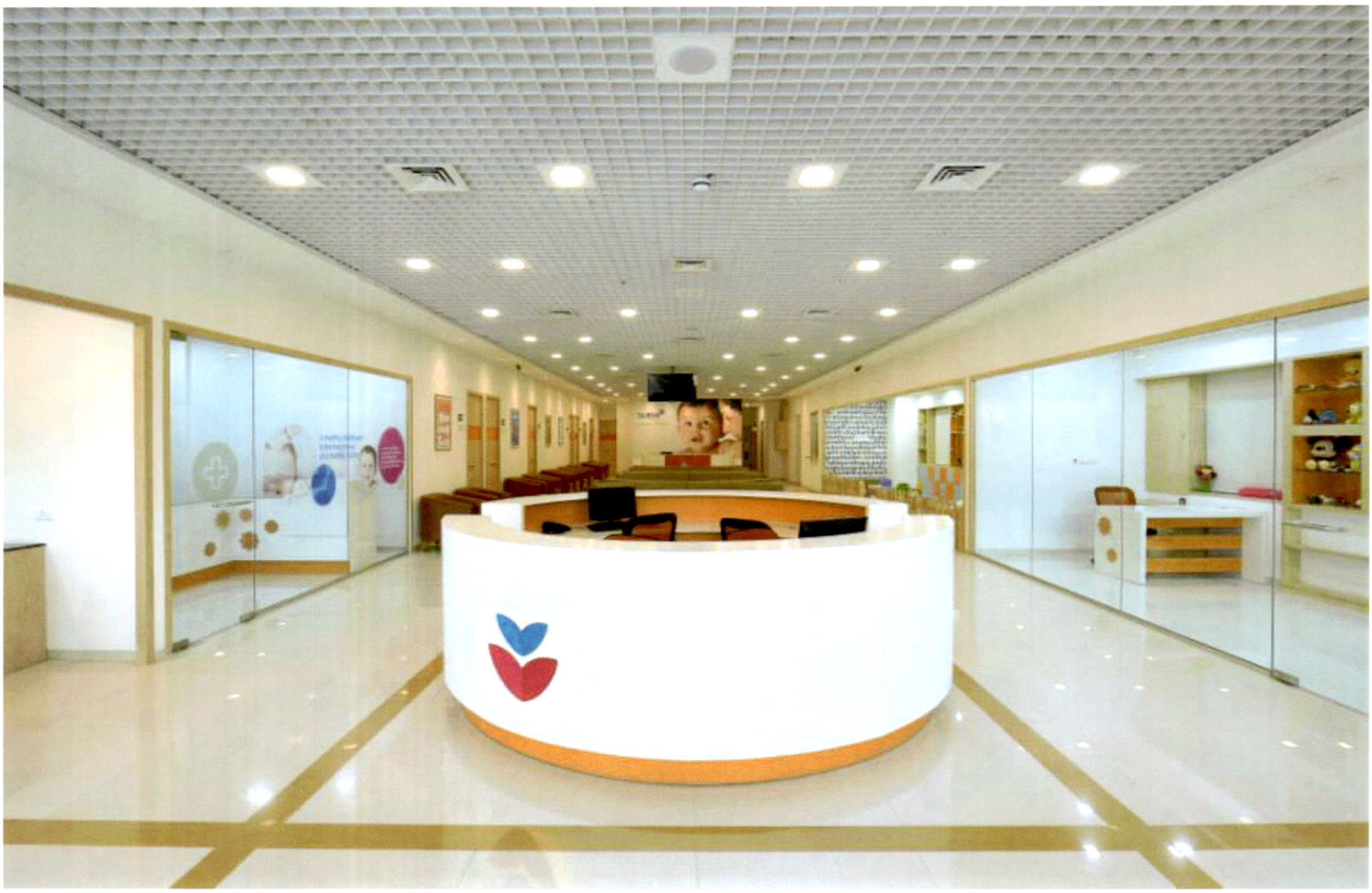

To make Surya Child Care a highly professional, safe, caring and stress-free facility, the designers built an environment fostering healthy living and child development. Big, fresh wayfinding signs clearly and simply guide visitors throughout the space. It is infused with charming, childlike graphics, with the intention of interacting with the kid and gaining the trust of parents. This design visualizes Surya's ethos and vision, while complimenting the architecture and building a trustworthy and humanistic environment.

Design Firm: Leaf Design **Designer:** Sandeep Ozarde, Prayag Shah **Photographer:** Prayag Shah **Client:** Surya Child Care **Location:** Mumbai, India

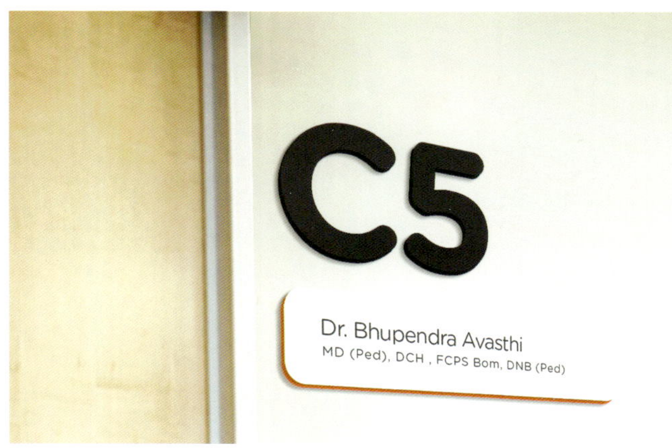

Size comparision and Placement

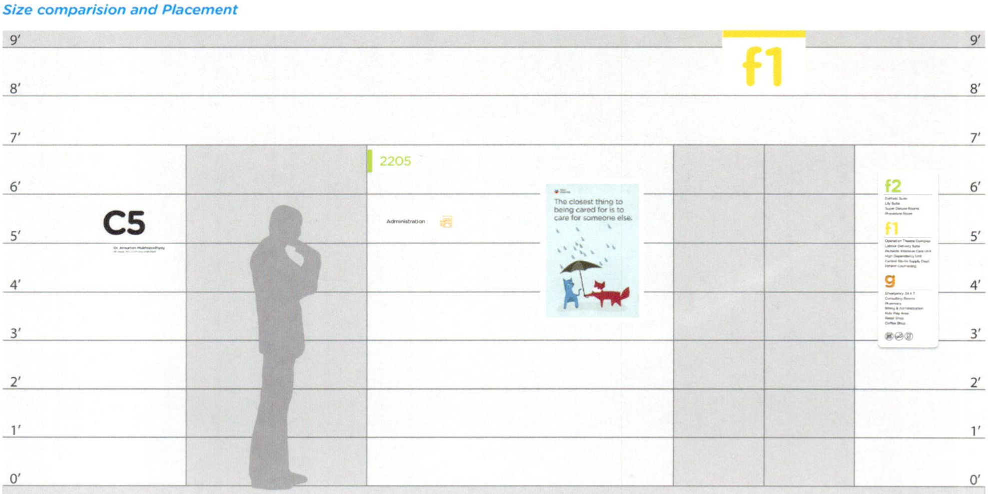

A Better A&E

Design Firm: PearsonLloyd **Directive Designer:** Tom Lloyd **Photographer:** Simon Turner Photography **Client:** Design Council and Department of Health **Location:** UK

Commissioned by the Design Council and Department of Health, the design team aimed to create a signage system to reduce levels of violence and aggression towards frontline hospital staff. A communication package including signage, leaflets and digital platforms was consequently designed to inform and guide patients through their time in the hospital.

A process map forms the core of this guidance solution. It depicts the entire A&E process as a series of stages with a pause between each one. From panels installed throughout the department, patients always know their locations and the stage of care availabel.

These panels were designed to have a clear hierarchy of information, with key information located at the top in the largest font sizes. Secondary and supplementary information is located below, in decreased font sizes. Projected to have a graphic aesthetic, the signage looks fresh and inviting, drawing patients to read the information. "Frutiger" was chosen as the font because of its legible sanserif font and moderate authority. Yellow icons were developed to communicate the right message to patients in a simple and easily understandable way.

This signage system results in an amicable appearance and expresses the objective of providing considerate services. It breaks the tension and greatly benefits patients as well as hospital staff.

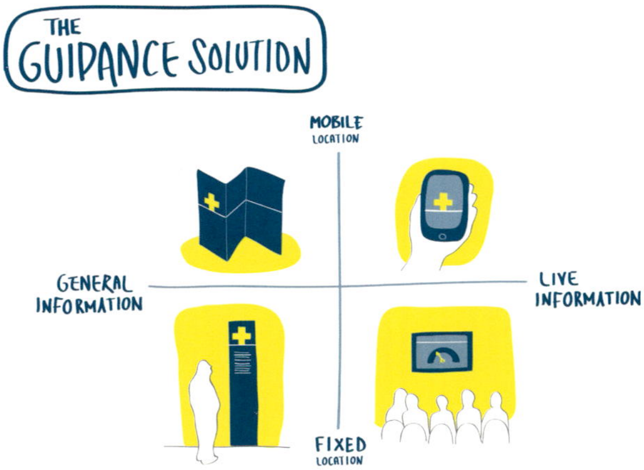
THE GUIDANCE SOLUTION
MOBILE LOCATION
GENERAL INFORMATION
LIVE INFORMATION
FIXED LOCATION

My NHS
NHS
A&E Department
Self Assessment
Local healthcare centres
A&E
Care pathways
Your history
Back
A&E
Back
St Fiction hospital
NHS
A&E Department
Normal
Quiet
Busy
Directions
Call A&E

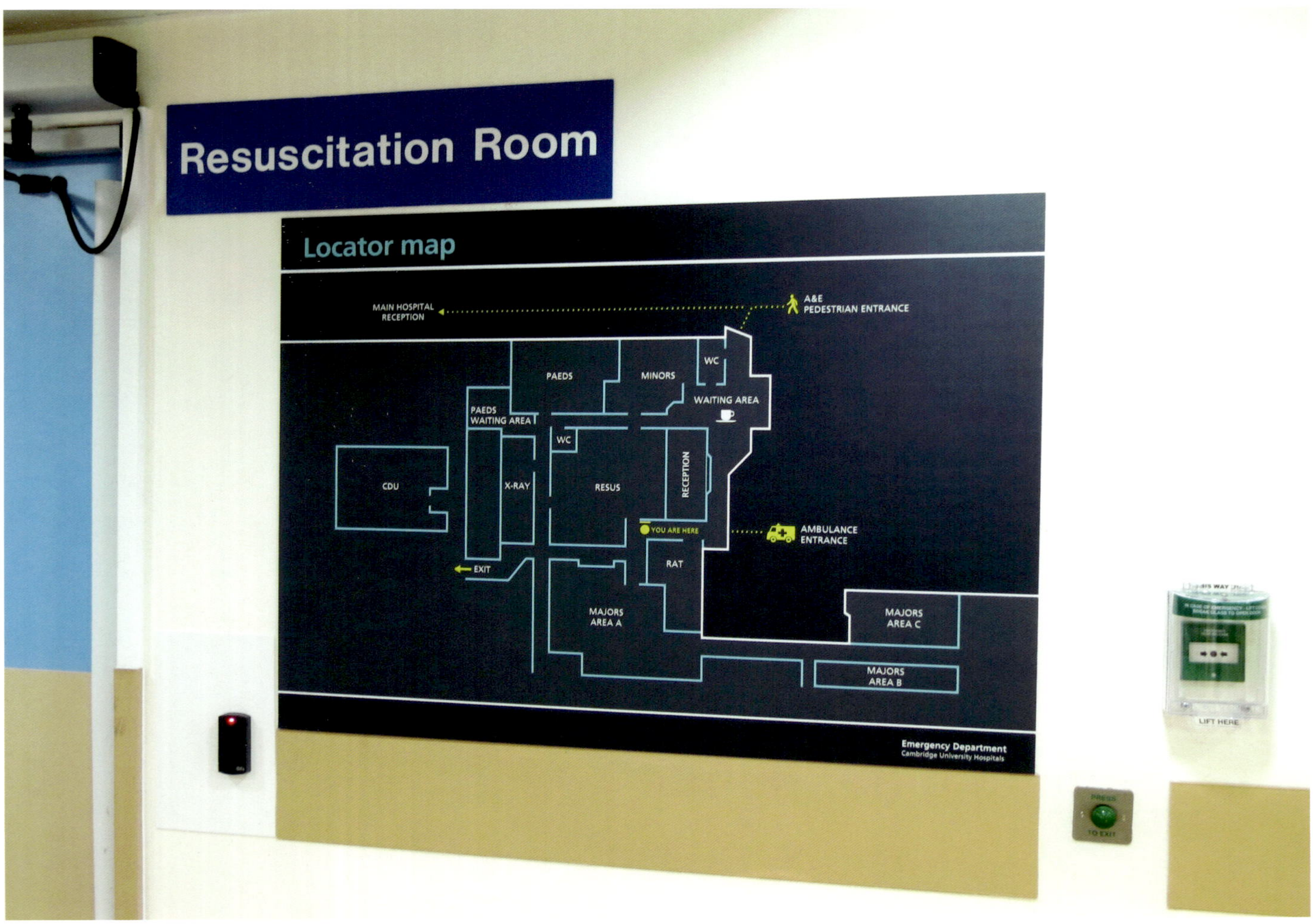
Resuscitation Room
Locator map
MAIN HOSPITAL RECEPTION
A&E PEDESTRIAN ENTRANCE
PAEDS
MINORS
WC
WAITING AREA
PAEDS WAITING AREA
WC
CDU
X-RAY
RESUS
RECEPTION
YOU ARE HERE
AMBULANCE ENTRANCE
EXIT
RAT
MAJORS AREA A
MAJORS AREA C
MAJORS AREA B
Emergency Department
Cambridge University Hospitals

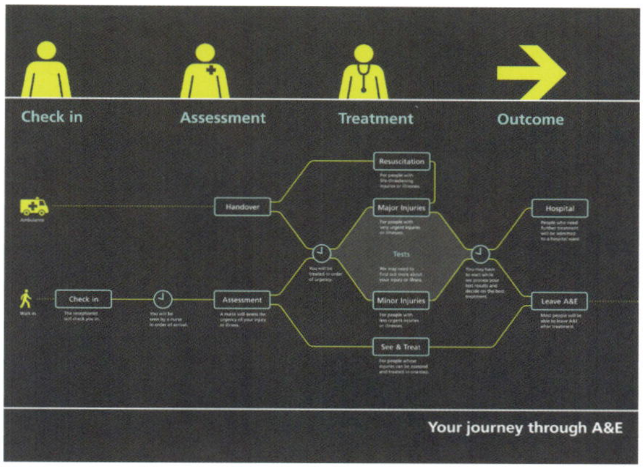
Check in
Assessment
Treatment
Outcome
Resuscitation
Handover
Major Injuries
Hospital
Tests
Check in
Assessment
Minor Injuries
Leave A&E
See & Treat
Your journey through A&E

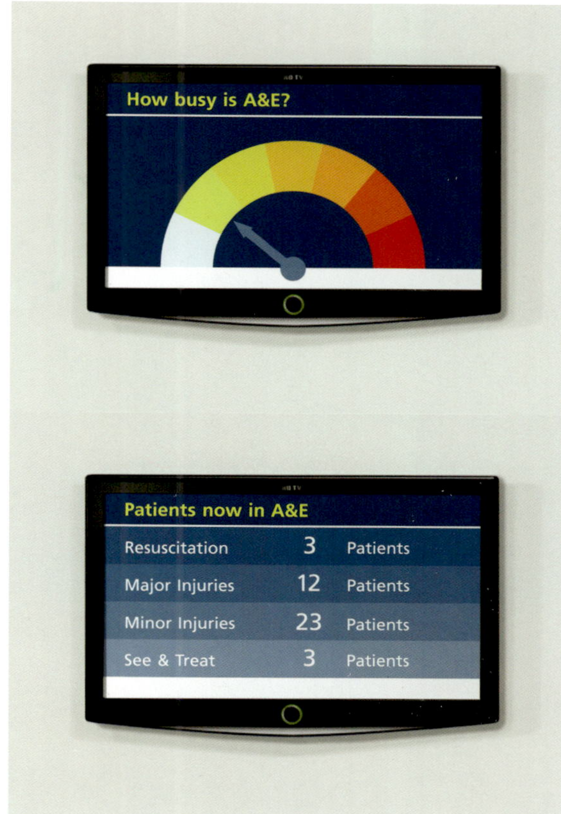
How busy is A&E?
Patients now in A&E
Resuscitation 3 Patients
Major Injuries 12 Patients
Minor Injuries 23 Patients
See & Treat 3 Patients

Resus 3
11:36

Offenbach Hospital

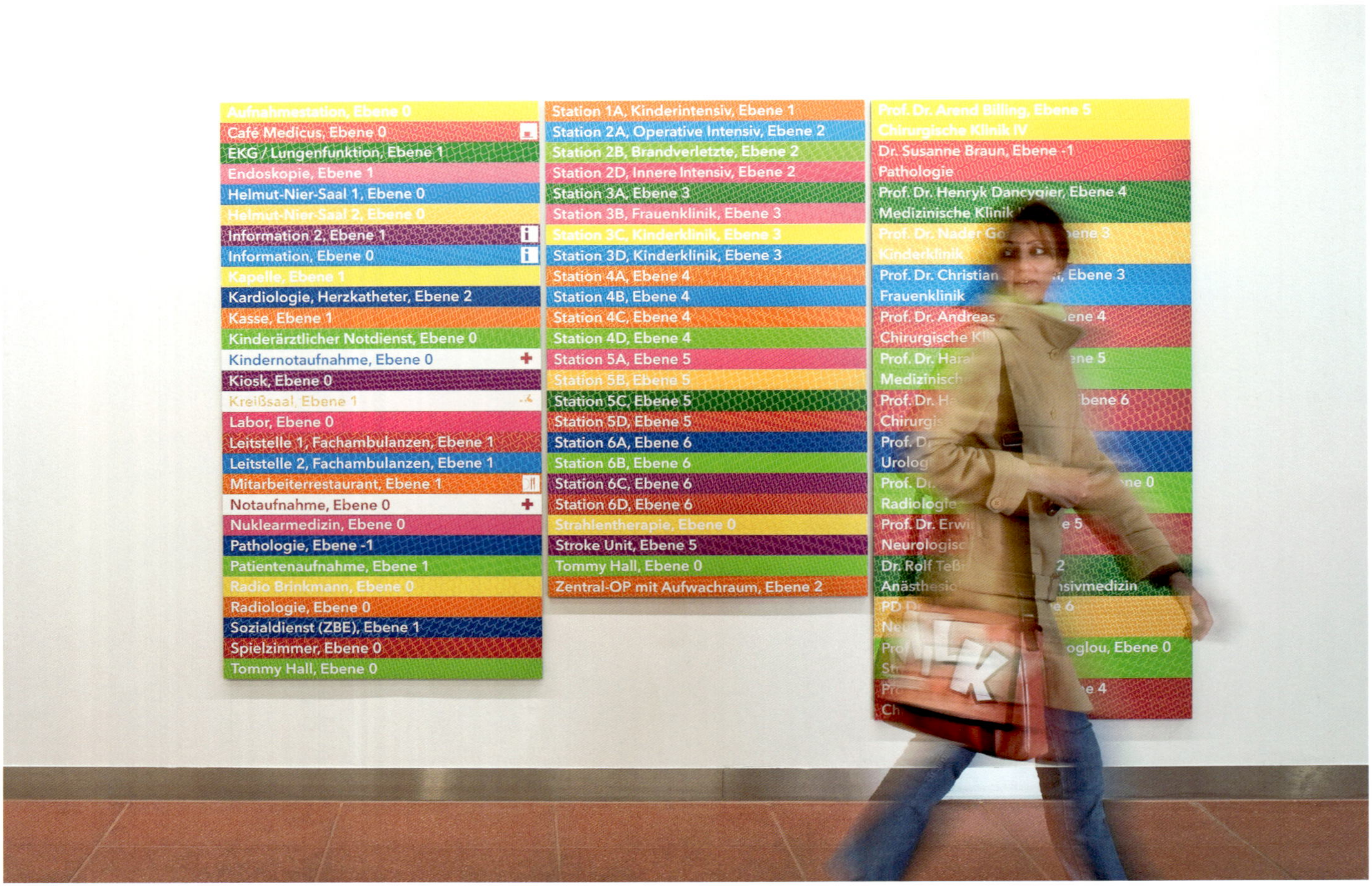

In Offenbach hospital, each area possesses an exclusive color and graphic pattern. Signage strips on the walls relay to visitors the color/pattern combination of their destinations; visitors visually memorize this design which guides them through the hospital complex. The reception areas are decorated by colorful wallpapers with patterns in identical designs on the counters and doors. Visual coding gives each location its own flavor. Colored geometrical patterns actively guide visitors and lighten the mood in the hospital.

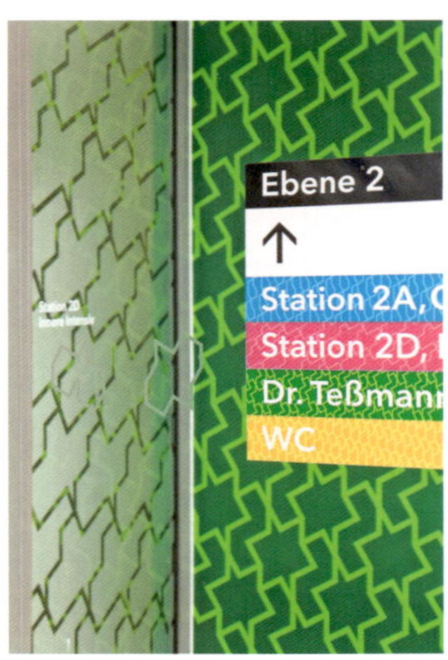

Design Firm: büro uebele visuelle kommunikation **Designer:** Katrin Theile, Andreas Uebele **Architect:** woernerundpartner **Photographer:** Andreas Körner
Client: woernerundpartner **Location:** Offenbach, Germany

Café Medicus
Information
Kindernotaufnahme
Notaufnahme
WC
Aufnahmestation
Helmut-Nier-Saal 1
Helmut-Nier-Saal 2
Kinderärztlicher Notdienst
Kiosk
Labor
Nuklearmedizin
Radio Brinkmann
Radiologie
Prof. Dr. Rilinger MBA
Strahlentherapie
Tommy Hall
Prof. Dr. Dr. Zamboglou

The Radiological Practice

Design Firm: büro uebele visuelle kommunikation **Designer:** Daniel Fels, Benedikt Haid, Andreas Uebele **Architect:** ZieglerBürg Büro für Gestaltung
Photographer: Andreas Körner **Client:** Dr. Stefan Heinrich, Dr. Esther Heinrich **Location:** Stuttgart, Germany

Signage in this medical institution is placed inside a series of variegated circles painted on the walls like ripples. Brightly-colored circles welcome patients and guide them all the way to their destinations, while lightening their mood and easing their fears.

5
6
7

5
7

WC
Personal

Women and Children's Hospital

Signage in adolescent wards of this hospital is presented in a clear and neat style to easily orient the patient. Combined with cozy interior colors and amusing graphics which provide encouragements for adolescents undergoing treatments, the signage reinforces a warm and cheerful atmosphere.

Design Firm: Prana Studios **Designer:** Hellen Kiprizloglou **Client:** Women and Children's Hospital **Location:** Adelaide, Australia

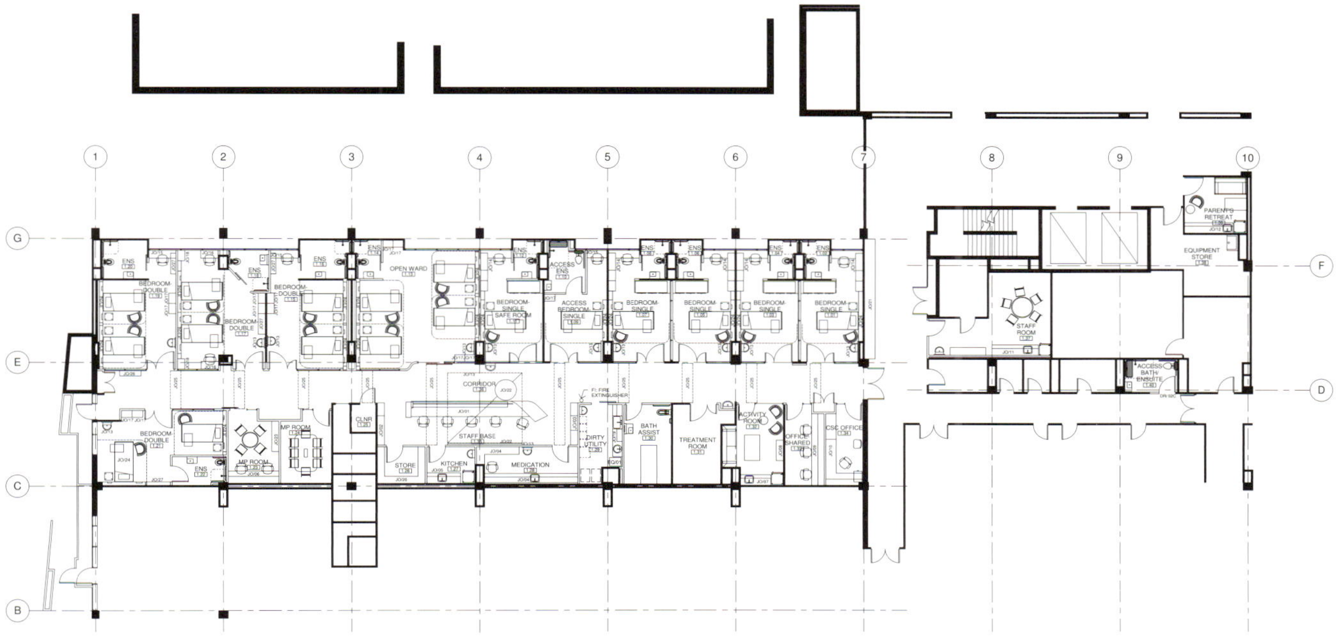

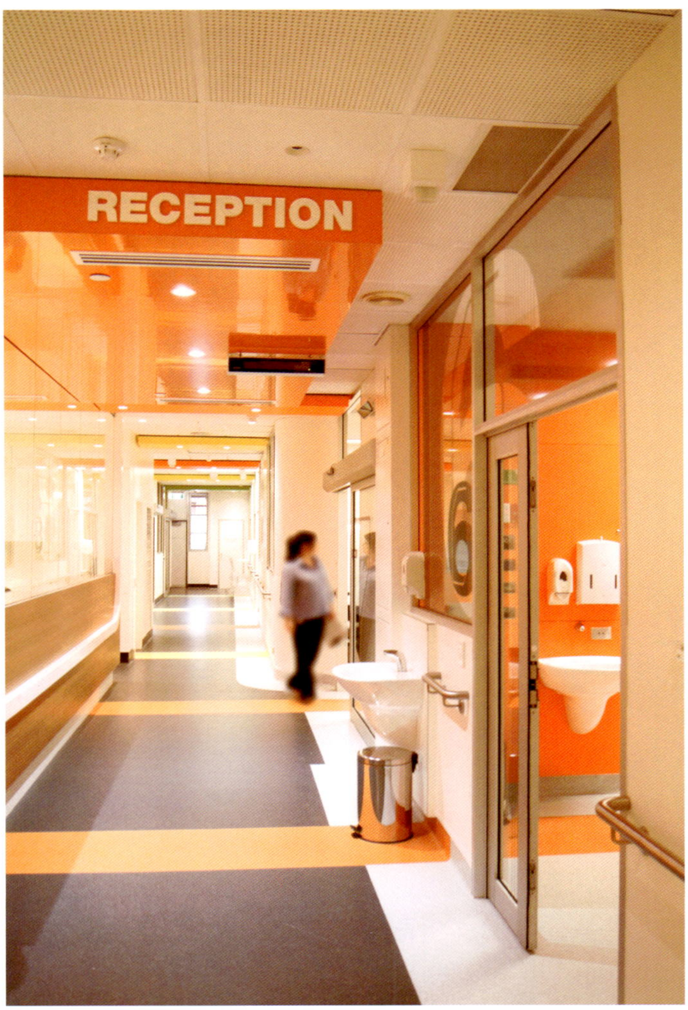
RECEPTION

HOPE

UNIMED Well-Being House

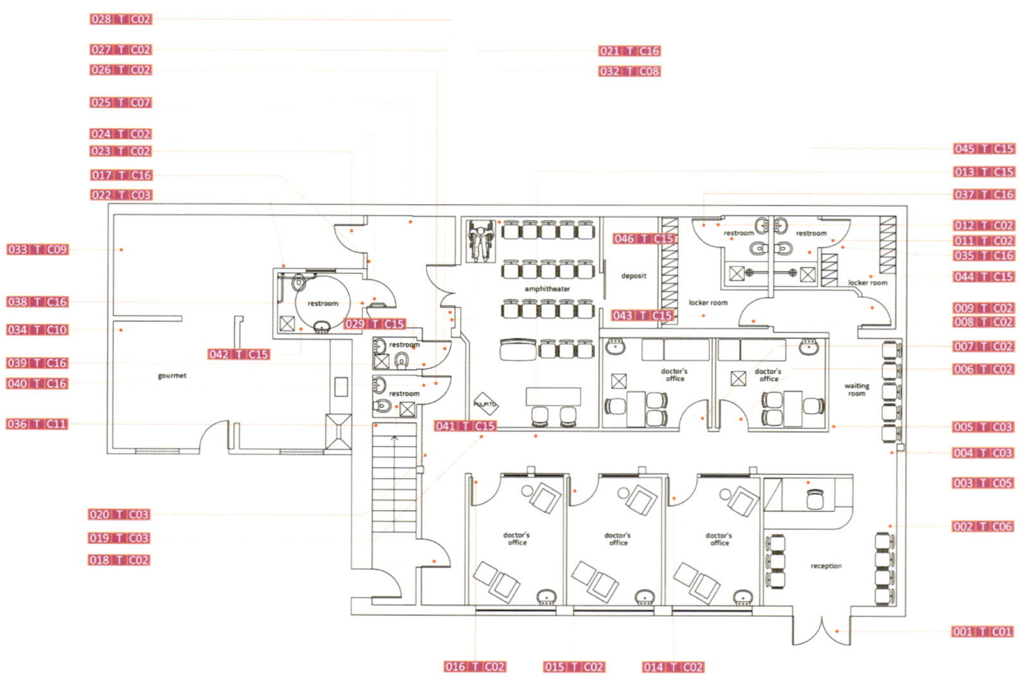

Design Firm: /STUDIOMDA **Designer:** Luciana Mattiello and /STUDIOMDA team **Photographer:** Marcelo Donadussi **Client:** UNIMED **Location:** Porto Alegre, RS, Brazil

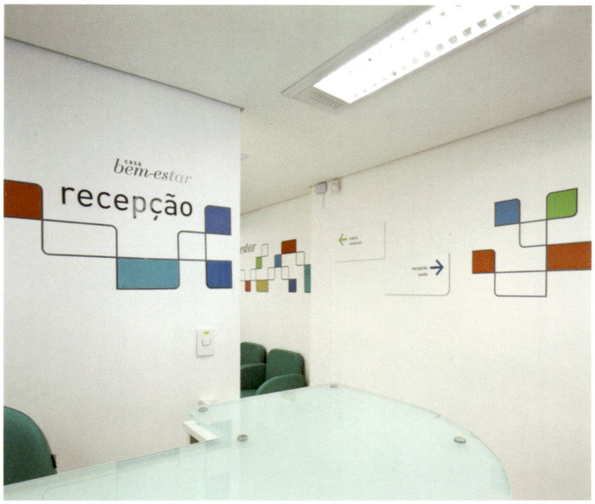
casa
bem-estar
recepção

sanitário
feminino

casa
bem-estar
recepção

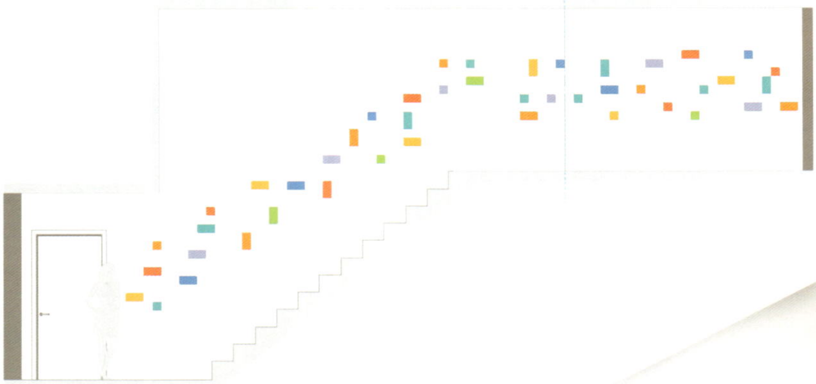

The signage design of Brazil's largest medical assistance institution is based on a chronological representation of life. Modular graphics and continuous colorful bands along the wall stand for the timeline. The wayfinding is incorporated within this stretching pattern to consistently offer information. With gentle and pleasant colors, the signage system strengthens hospitality and warm feelings in the medical environment.

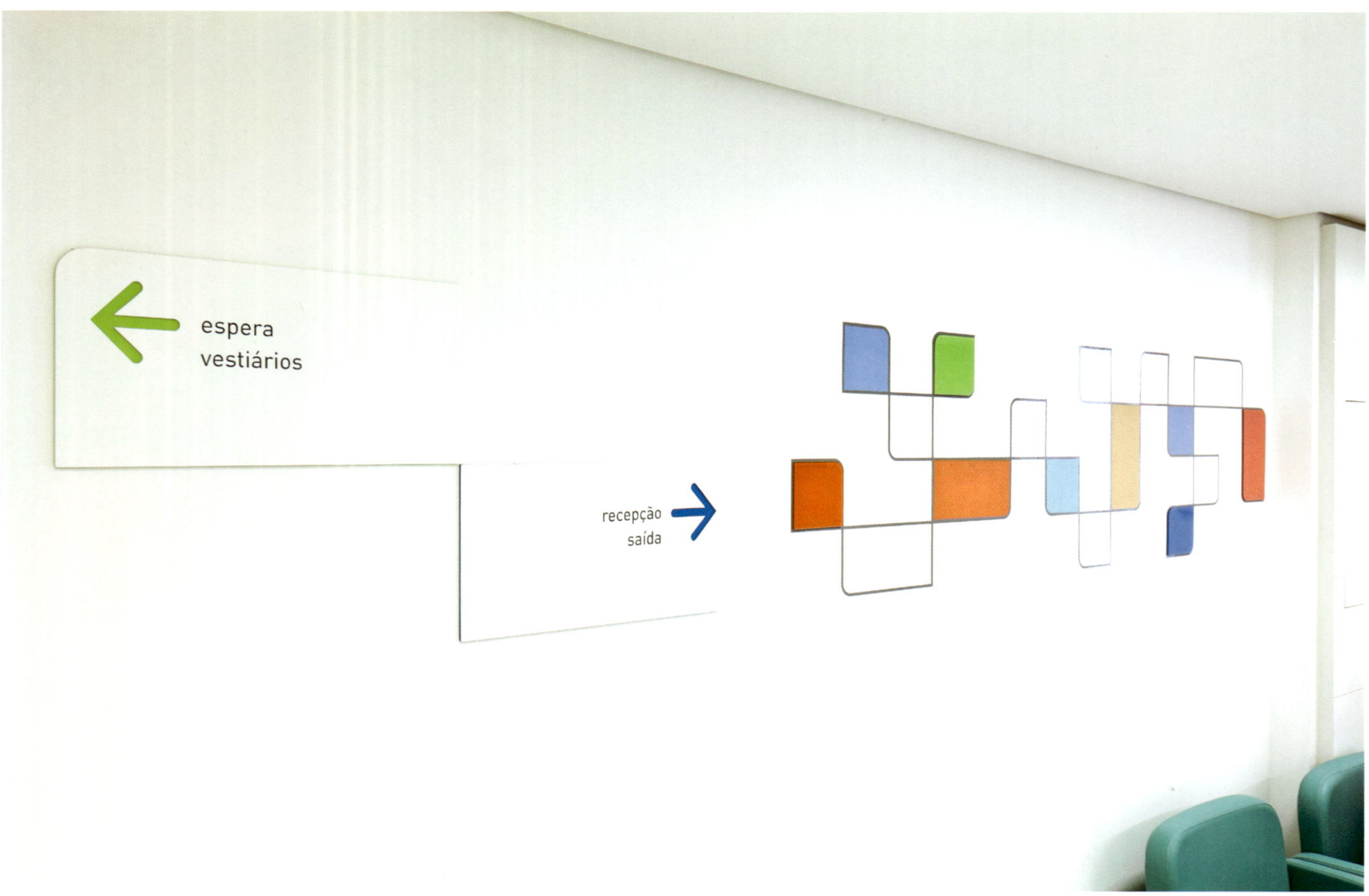

sala de espera

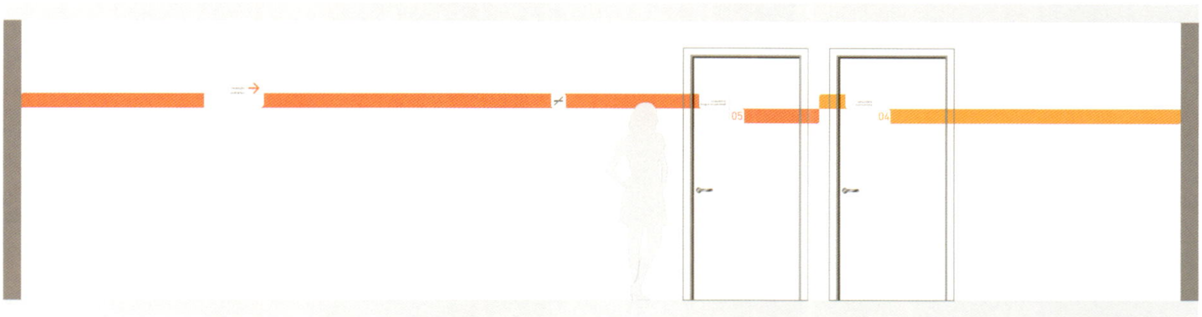

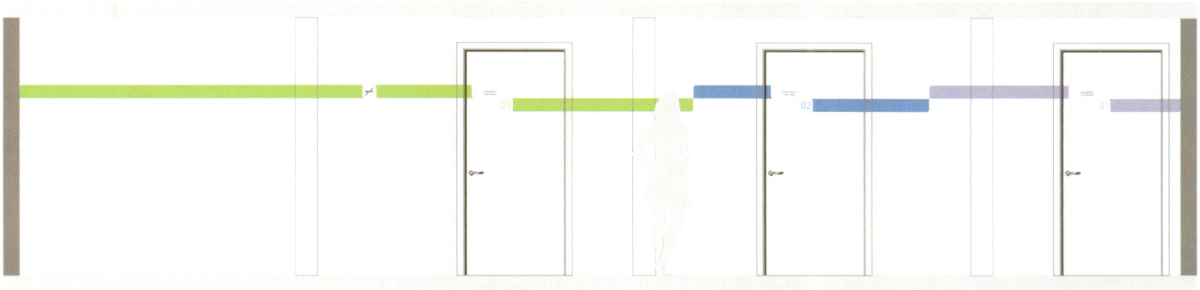

Silesian Hospital

In the signage project of Silesian hospital, the designer created a tailored font with regular and light variants. A set of pictograms was designed in a mellow, neat style. The information boards outside the building use brown for the background with florescent effects to lead people at night. This sign system consistently assists people in need and its modest appearance gives the hospital a trustworthy image.

Designer: Iwona Przybyła **Photographer:** Iwona Przybyla **Client:** Silesian hospital **Location:** Cieszyn, Poland

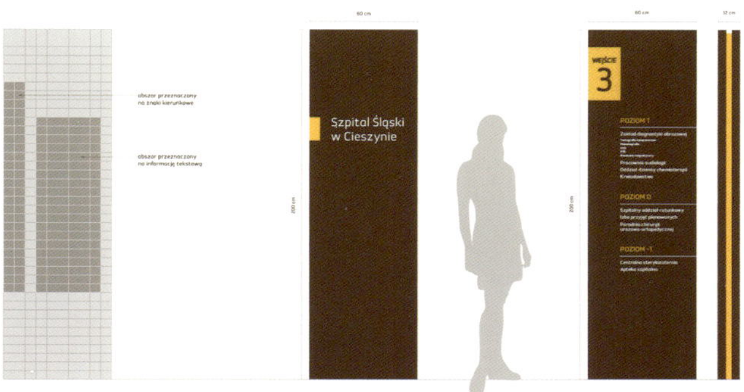
Szpital Śląski
w Cieszynie
3
POZIOM 1
POZIOM 0
POZIOM -1

BUDYNEK
B
PARKING

Izba przyjęć
Opieka
Nocna i Świąteczna
Wejście główne
Zespół poradni
specjalistycznych
Dzienny oddział
psychiatryczny
Poradnia zdrowia
psychicznego

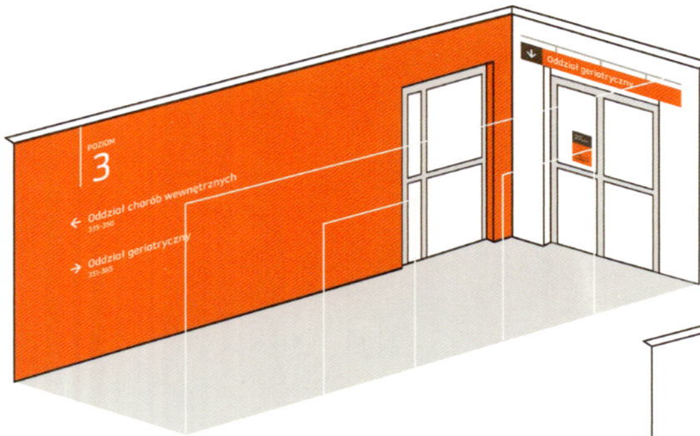
POZIOM
3
Oddział chorób wewnętrznych
Oddział geriatryczny
Oddział geriatryczny

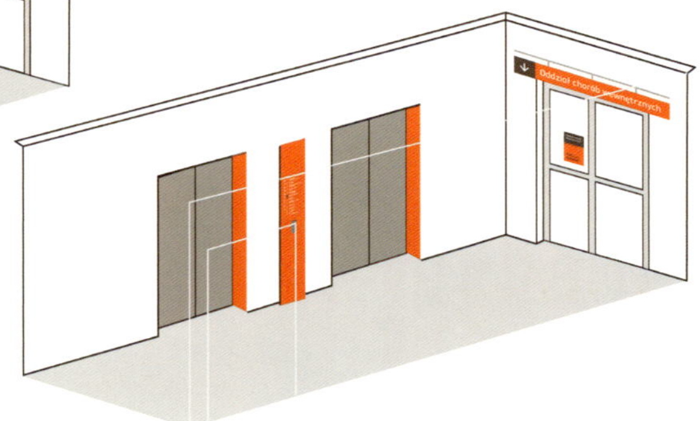
Oddział chorób wewnętrznych

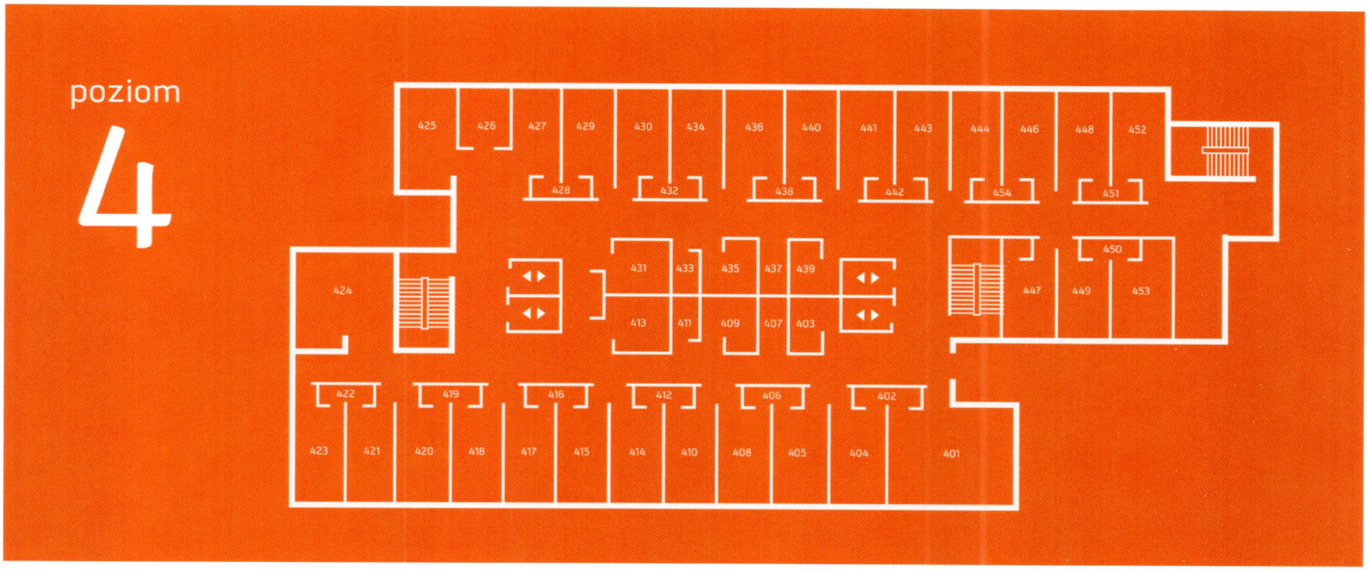
poziom
4

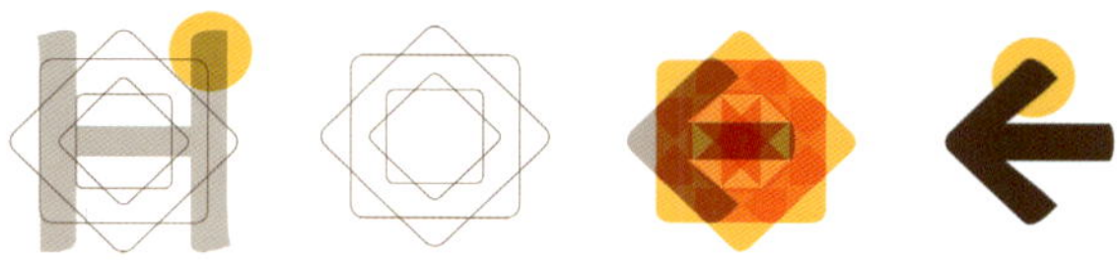

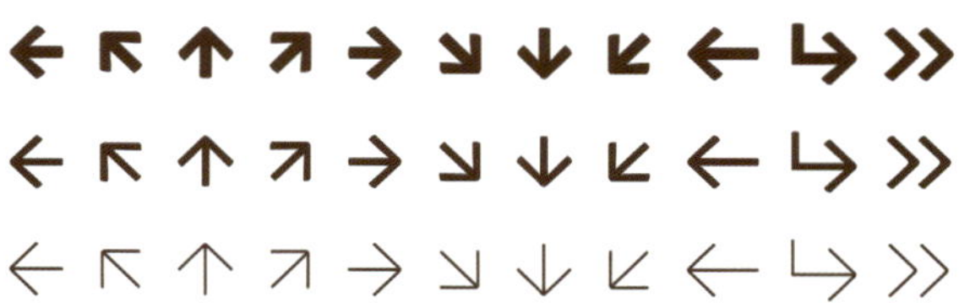

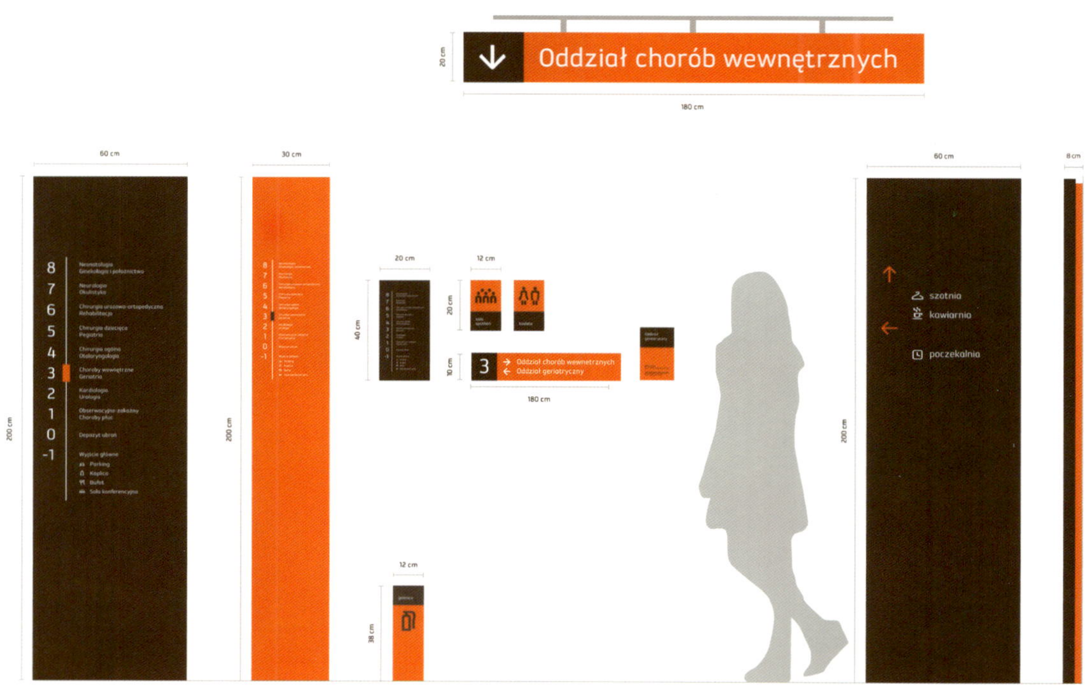
Oddział chorób wewnętrznych
20 cm
180 cm
60 cm
30 cm
200 cm
szatnia
kawiarnia
poczekalnia

Westerdals

A special typeface named "Shadow" was created for the signage system in the media library of Westerdals School of Communication. The letters and numbers are united with shadows, constituting functional and aesthetic wayfinding information. The floor number signs were painted on the wall by hand in large red figures to make the guidance stand out or pop on grey backgrounds; original floorboards and glass windows act as a canvas for the bright signage. This sign system easily navigates students and complements the decoration. It adds modern and technical elements to this rough and industrial architecture. The shadows linking information are a metaphor for the relationship between the library and students: the interaction between inspiration and creation.

Designer: Marius Holtmon, Mette Landsem, Madeleine Skjelland Eriksen **Photographer:** Marius Holtmon, Mette Landsem, Madeleine Skjelland Eriksen
Client: Westerdals **Location:** Oslo, Norway

221

INFO

4
ART DIRECTION
TEKST & SKRIBENT
EXPERIENCE & EVENT
3
FILM & TV
GRAFISK DESIGN
EKSPONERINGSDESIGN
2
ADMIN
ANSATTE
MØTEROM
1
KANTINE
MEDIATEK
RESEPSJON
0
ATELIER
VERKSTED
AUDITORIUM

ADMINISTRASJON
TEKNOLOGI
ADMINISTRASJON
LEDELSE
UTDANNING
PEDAGOGIKK
KOMMUNIKASJON
SPRÅK
TEKNOLOGI
TYPOGRAFI
KUNST
ARKITEKTUR
EKSPONERINGSDESIGN
SAMFUNNSVITENSKAP
KULTUR
GRAFISK DESIGN

MED
IA
TEKET

2
ADMIN
ANSATTE
MØTEROM

4
ART DIRECTION
TEKST & SKRIBENT
EXPERIENCE & EVENT
3
FILM & TV
GRAFISK DESIGN
EKSPONERINGSDESIGN

AUDITORIUM

IPAM

With the intention to create a direct and active communication between Portuguese marketing school IPAM and its visitors, oversized signage information is applied. Big black lettering painted on the wall causes the building to speak directly to those people passing by. The signage system is effective, delivering an invitation of interaction between its target audience and the institution, and visually strengthening the school's identity.

Design Firm: P-06 Atelier **Designer:** Nuno Gusmão, Mário Videira **Photographer:** IADE, P-06 Atelier **Client:** IPAM **Location:** Oporto, Portugal

HELLO,
CAN I HELP YOU?

READ THIS
PLEASE...
BIBLIOTECA
PISO 2

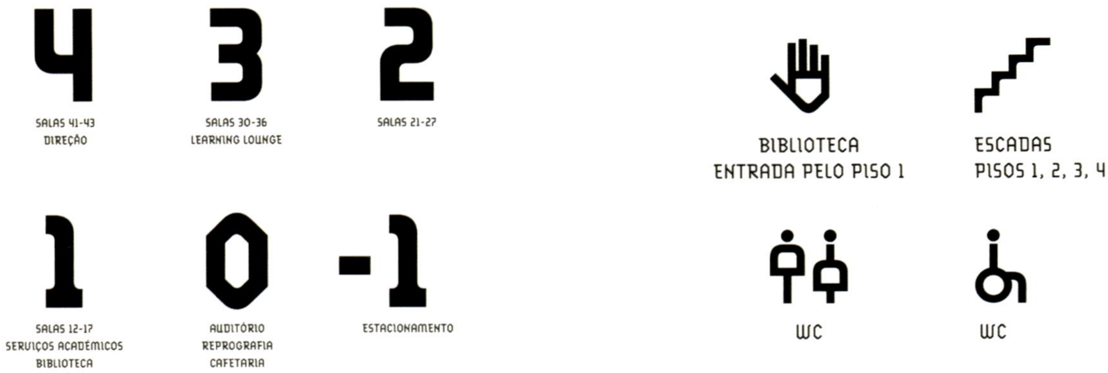

4
SALAS 41-43
DIREÇÃO
3
SALAS 30-36
LEARNING LOUNGE
2
SALAS 21-27
1
SALAS 12-17
SERVIÇOS ACADÉMICOS
BIBLIOTECA
0
AUDITÓRIO
REPROGRAFIA
CAFETARIA
-1
ESTACIONAMENTO
BIBLIOTECA
ENTRADA PELO PISO 1
ESCADAS
PISOS 1, 2, 3, 4
WC
WC

11
SERVIÇOS ACADÉMICOS

AUDITÓRIO

REPROGRAFIA
SALAS 21-27
WC
AUDITÓRIO
CAFETARIA
WC
SALAS DE AULA
DIREÇÃO
LEARNING LOUNGE
BIBLIOTECA
SERVIÇOS ACADÉMICOS

14
11

RMIT Swanston Academic Building

Design Firm: Büro North **Designer:** Jess Caffin, Giovanni Mendini, Gary Pennington, Tim Dow, Ben Ryan **Photographer:** Fraser Marsden **Client:** RMIT University
Location: Melbourne, Australia

The signage system in the academic building in Melbourne's CBD refers to the numerous of materials employed in its interior decoration. Oversized wayfinding information on the wall is prominent; the deep red ribbon-like signage form hangs from the ceiling, mimicking the traffic flows and articulating the signage information for each area. This sign system is a well-organized design that efficiently guides people through the area while maintaining information's clarity and legibility. It also coordinates with the building's interior design and helps shape a classy academic environment.

You are on Level 2
Upper levels
Business Central - Level 7
To Level 1
Cinema Theatre 80|1|02
Exit to Stewart Street

Cinema Theatre upper entry
Rooms 80|2|16 and 80|2|17
Exit to Swanston Street
Exit to Stewart Street
80|2|03
2

Cinema Theatre 80|1|02
Exit to Stewart Street
Exit to A'Beckett Street
Rooms 80|2|01 to 80|2|17
Exit to Swanston Street

8

Rooms 80|3|13 and 80|3|14
Building 81 - School of Graduate Research

Fundação Dom Cabral

The signage project developed for this business school implements the idea of pictograms disconnected from the walls so that they can be recognized from a distance. The simple icons jump out from their boards and provide vivid guidance. The design is in consonance with the school's vision of a holistic professional development directed towards the future, exceeding past aspirations and achieving new goals.

Design Firm: Greco Design **Designer:** Tidé, Ana Luiza Gomes, Fernanda Monte-Mór, Bruno Nunes, Daniele Pires, Flávia Siqueira **Photographer:** Rafa Motta
Client: Fundação Dom Cabral **Location:** Belo Horizonte, Brazil

ESTACIONAMENTO
PARKING LOT | ESTACIONAMIENTO
CARGA E DESCARGA
DELIVERY | CARGA Y DESCARGA

ESPAÇO MULTIUSO
MULTI-USE SPACE
ESPACIO MULTIUSO
3
SALA
ROOM | SALA

INDOOR PUBLIC SPACE

Wayfinding in Indoor Public Spaces: An Animating Journey

Indoor public spaces, such as indoor carparks, airports, shopping malls and stores, are often characterized by vast open areas, a large flow of people, or a feast of background colors.

In parking lots, where motorists hunger for clear directions, the top priority of the signage design is to build a system that effectively guides. In addition to successfully fulfilling their navigational functions, the wayfinding graphics serve as an intriguing decorating element to visually stimulate those who drive into this space.

The clarity of wayfinding system is equally important in retail sector as consumers are faced with dazzling showcases and intricate routes. The main challenge for signage design comes in shopping malls: signs have to jump out of the background and stably lead the way. Meanwhile, as a wayfinding system faciliates customers through their shopping experiences, it produces more benefits for the malls if it caters to the interior architectural style and fosters an impressive brand personality.

Korona Kielce Mall

The signage structure for this shopping center includes a complete visual information system along with 3D media, info graphics, multimedia elements and a parking guide. Three parking levels use multicolored, raster wallpapers with diverse graphics to visually distinguish the levels and liven up the walls of the corridors. Signage is shown on prominent boards with further detailed information accessible on touch screens. The information counters were designed with the use of Corian. Owing to the unique construction properties of this material, the signage equipments created is light and self-supporting, responding to the architectural structure. Integrated with the distinct interior design, this signage system gives the center a fresh, feminine vibe, and helps to make shopping enjoyable by providing a pleasant way-finding experience with a relaxing walk.

Design Firm: DODOPLAN **Designer:** Dorota Januszek, Izabela Brola, Honorata Poznanska, Robert Mieniok **Photographer:** Dorota Januszek **Client:** MGC Inwest
Location: Kielce, Poland

ŁAZIENKA POZIOM 0
podkład 0 rozowy . tiff
podkład 0 lacznik . tiff
podkład 0 niebieski . tiff
Szczególną uwagę należy zwrócić na fakt, że grafika „Bocian" znaleźć się powinna we wnęce, nad ławką
sugerowana kolejność wyklejania

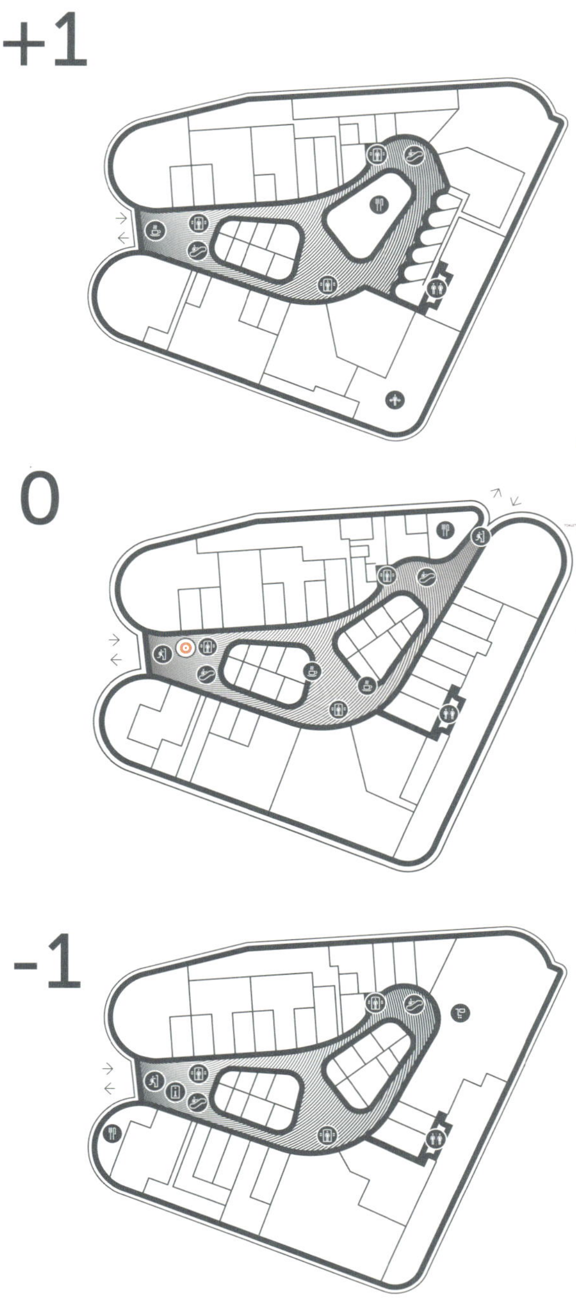
+1
0
-1

KORONA
GALERIA KIELCE
4P
3P
2P
+1
0
-1
-2
KORONA
GALERIA KIELCE
+1
0
-1
-2

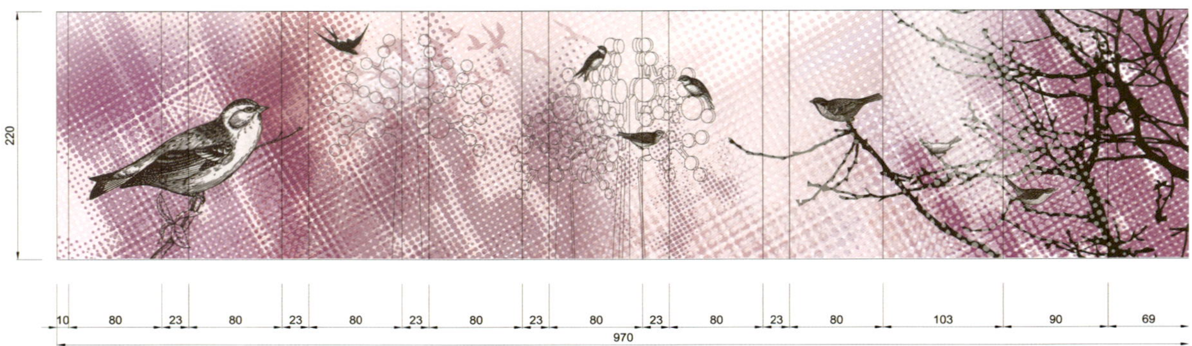

220
10
80
23
80
23
80
23
80
23
80
23
80
23
80
103
90
69
970

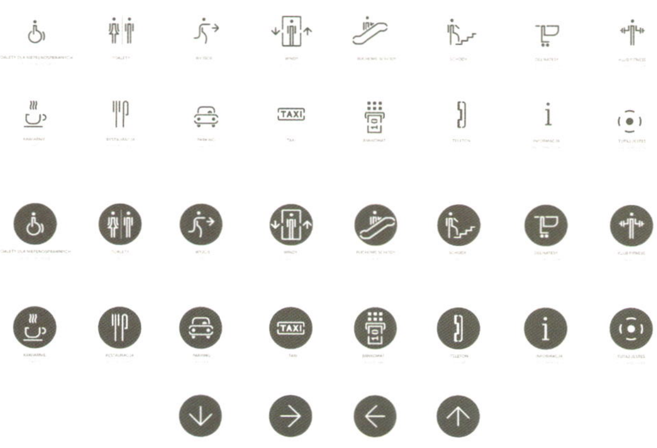
TAXI
TAXI

0
POZIOM
LEVEL
POZIOM
LEVEL
-1
POZIOM
LEVEL
-2
ul. Polna

7
6
5
4
3
2
1
Wejście

JA Minds

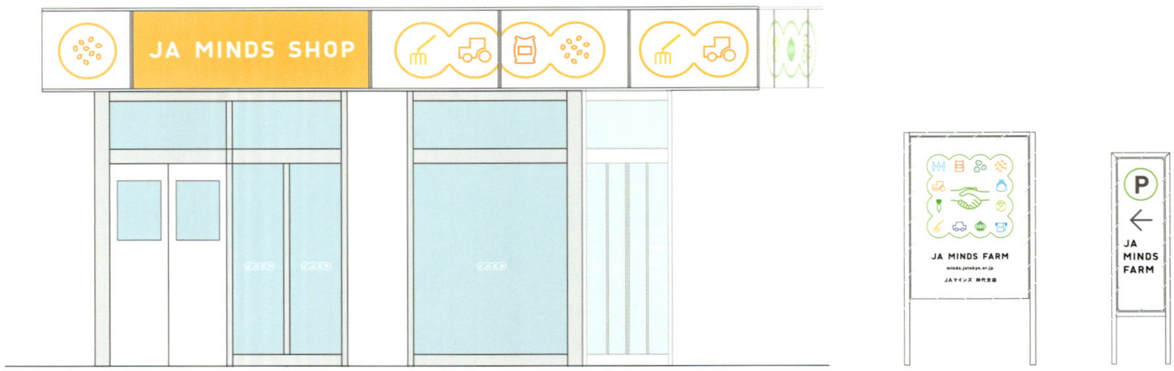

JA Minds is a chain store under Japan Agricultural Cooperatives. With the intention of creating a brilliant communication platform for customers, the designer associated the signage system with the visual identity of JA Minds. A series of pictograms were created in mild colors and genial images. The pictograms build an affinity between the signage and the brand image, and instantly communicate JA's services to a wide target group, delivering concepts of ecological agriculture and organic farming.

Design Firm: 6D-K **Designer:** Shogo Kishino, Nozomi Tagami **Photographer:** Shingo Fujimoto **Client:** Minds Agricultural Cooperative **Location:** Tokyo, Japan

JA MINDS
JA MINDS FRESH
JA MINDS FRESH

P
JA
MINDS
FARM

JA MINDS FARM
minds.jatokyo.or.jp
JAマインス 多磨支店

■ 屋外自立サイン ×5 台

B-1 店舗施設名称サイン（自立型 非内照）

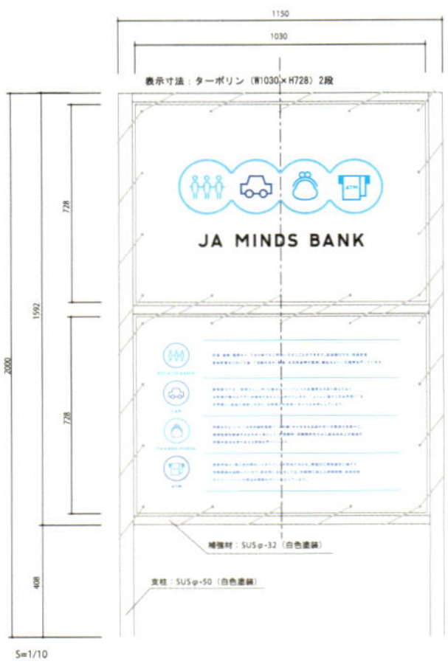

B-2 店舗施設名称サイン（自立型 非内照）

B-3 店舗施設名称サイン（自立型 非内照）

B-5a 外構 施設名称サイン（自立 非内照）

B-5b 店舗施設名称サイン（自立型 非内照）

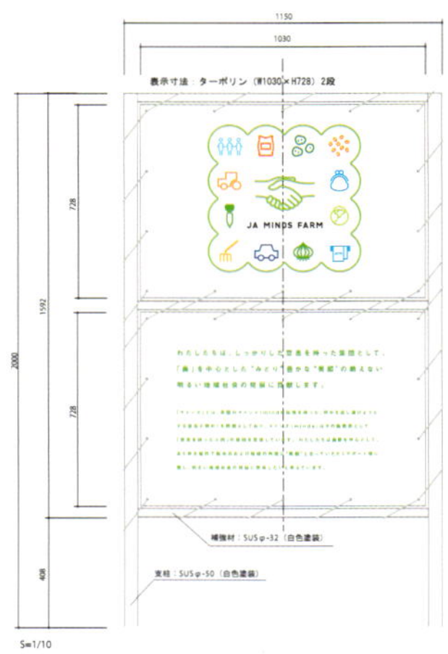

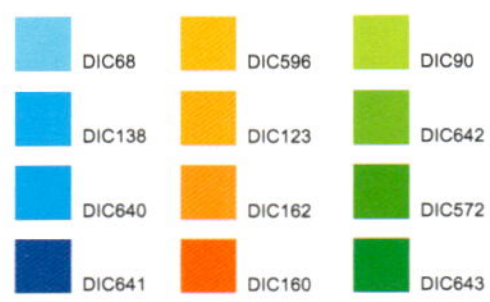

JA MINDS SHOP
JA MINDS FRESH

JA MINDS FARM
JA MINDS BANK
JA MINDS SHOP
JA MINDS FRESH
JA MINDS FARM
P
JA MINDS FARM

JA MINDS FARM
JA MINDS FARM
RSE RELATIONS
HIP ONION TR
ACTOR HOME S
PINACH RAKE
CASH WHITERAD
JA MINDS BANK
JA MINDS BANK
JA MINDS FARM
JA MINDS FRESH
JA MINDS SHOP
JA MINDS SHOP

Moinhos Shopping Mall

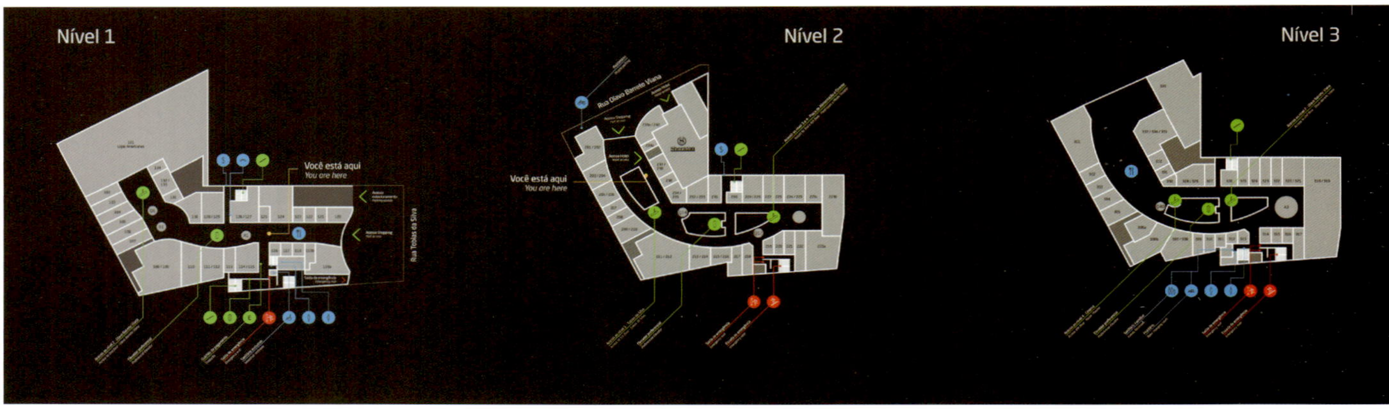

Design Firm: /STUDIOMDA **Designer:** Luciana Mattiello and /STUDIOMDA team **Photographer:** Marcelo Donadussi
Client: Pateo Moinhos de Vento Real Estate Investment Fund **Location:** Porto Alegre, RS, Brazil

This shopping mall adopts minimalist elements in its signage system. Four parking floors are distinguished by different color themes. Simple pictograms were created in the contrast between black and white. The designer used matte and glossy materials to highlight the sense of modernism. This easily-understandable, bilingual signage system functionally guides visitors through this complex, while emphasizing the brand's concept of rendering upscale services.

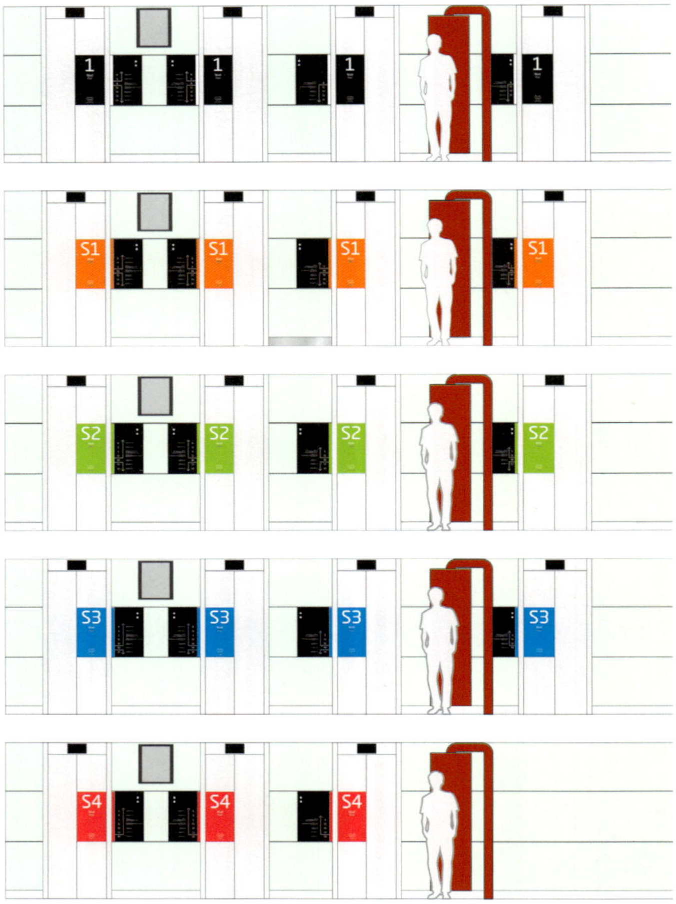
1
S1
S2
S3
S4

Sanitário Masculino
Sanitário Feminino
Sanitário Familiar
Sanitário Exclusivo

Sanitário Masculino | Men's Restroom

Sheraton Hotel
Praça de Alimentação
Food Court
Cinemas
Cinema
Sanitários
Toilets
2
Donna ly

2
LONDON CALLING
Exposição fotográfica de
ALBERTO MENEGHETTI

The Stone Towers

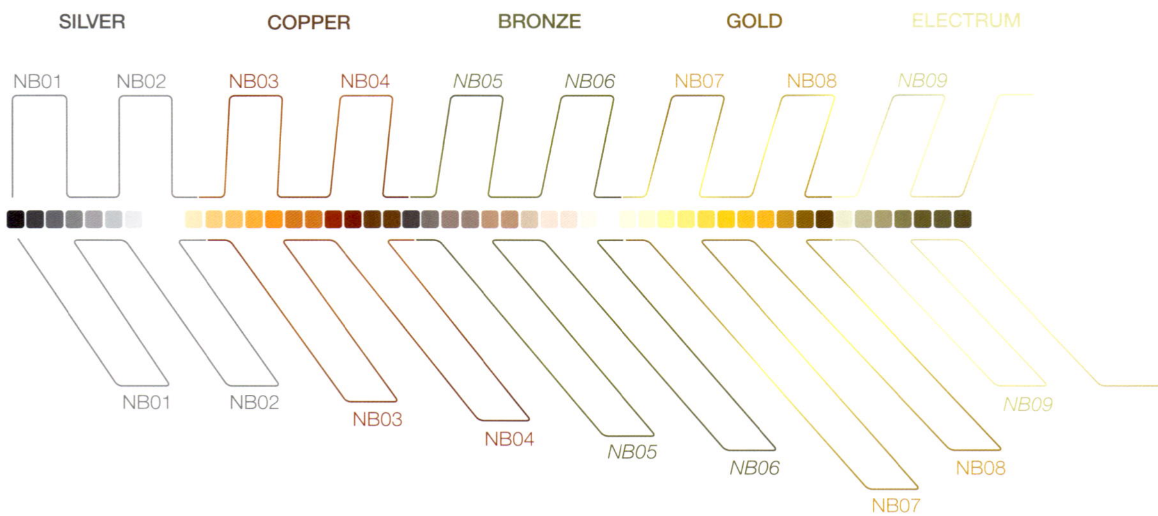

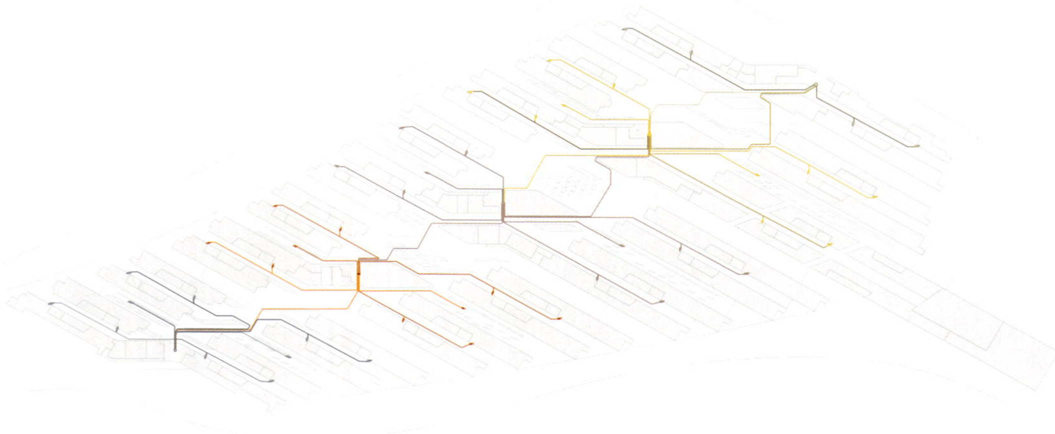

Stone Towers is a large multi-functional development in Cairo designed by Zaha Hadid Architects, consisting of commercial, retail, hotel, public spaces and parking areas. Based on a thorough understanding of the project's spatial system and framework for movement, the design team developed a signage system to enhance orientation. Inspired by the concept of "stratification" found in the site's geological context and in the architectural design from Zaha Hadid's team, the technique of engraving in stone and the hieroglyphic style of the pictographs are utilized in the signage to adapt the modern language of iconography to the local populace. In homage to the importance of metals in both the economic practices and religious beliefs of ancient Egyptians, five important metals - gold, silver, copper, bronze and electrum - are selected as identifying colors for the five retail zones and as the basic color tones throughout the signage system.

In the public areas, wayfinding bands are inlaid in the ground as illuminated, metallic indicators, marking the way to various destinations. These wayfinding bands all originate at an entrance from the car park, and lead to the building entrance. From this starting point, the bands continue on to key locations where the bands converge into diamond-shaped panels which contain information, and point the way toward several other destinations. Within the retail zones, signage panels are tightly integrated with into landscape and conceived by pulling up individual landscape strips to form the shop directories.

Design Firm: Space Agency **Designer:** Peter Feldmann, Sarah Manning, Charlotte Cohen and Bartosz Dudzikowski **Architect:** Zaha Hadid Architects
Client: Rooya Group **Location:** Cairo, Egypt

This systematic signage design facilitates orientation and leaves marvellous visual impressions on visitors. Sensory elements are used to express a visual identity and generate a better user experience. Embellished with modern as well as traditional Egyptian elements, the large space becomes navigable through an attractive and intuitive hierarchy of information revealed progressively throughout the visitor's journey.

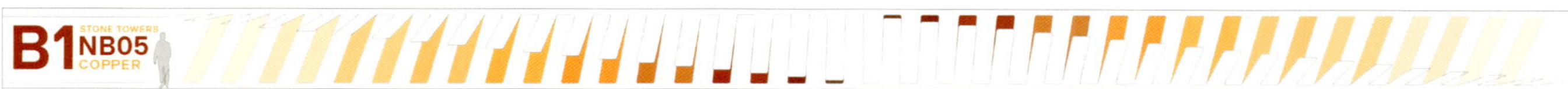

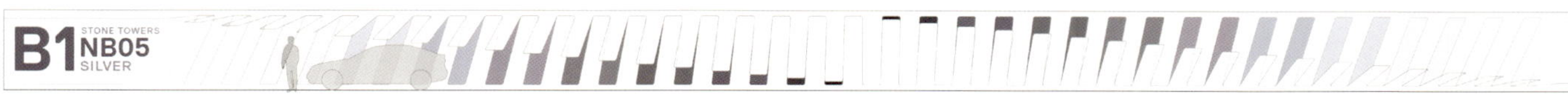

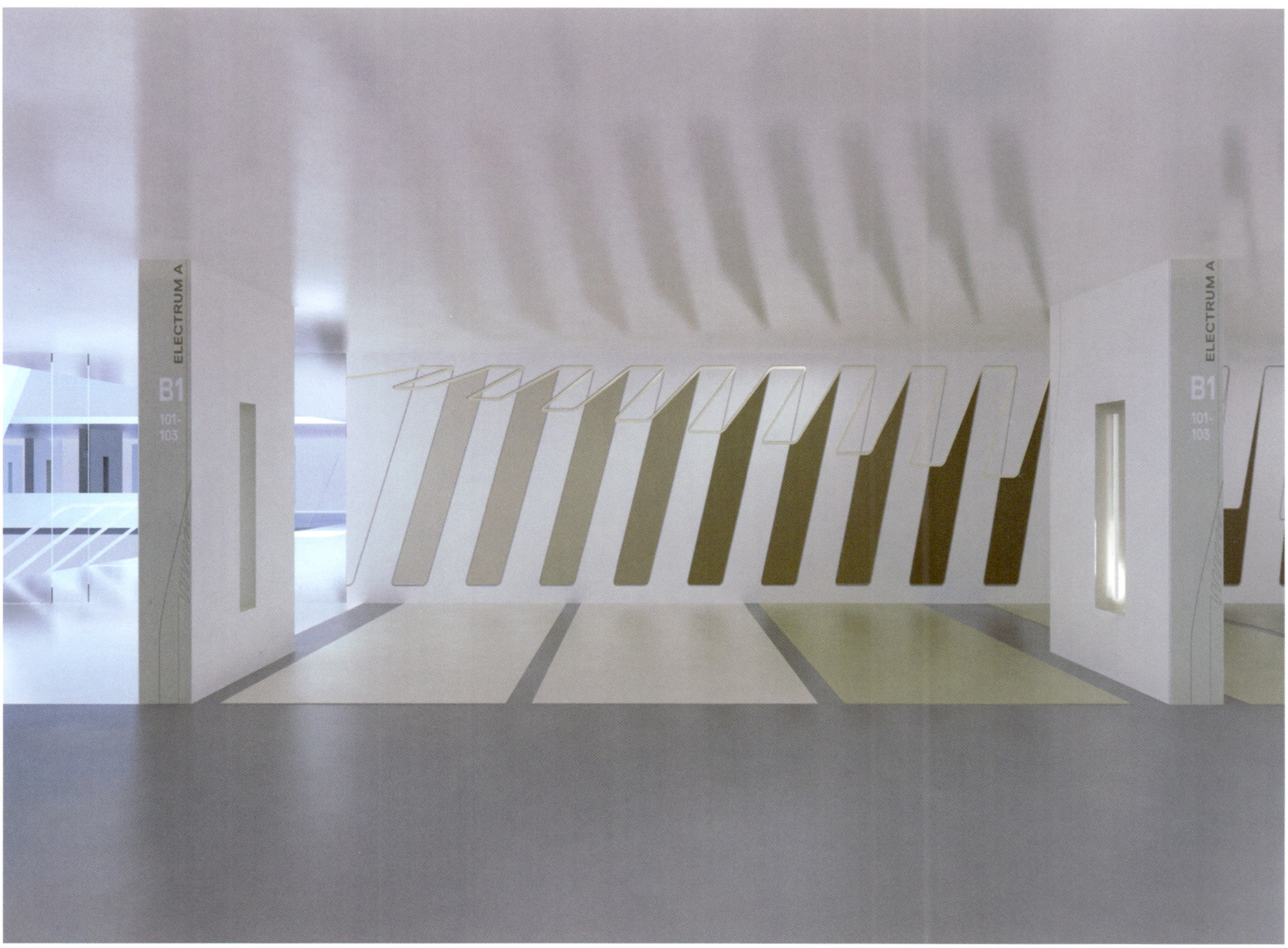

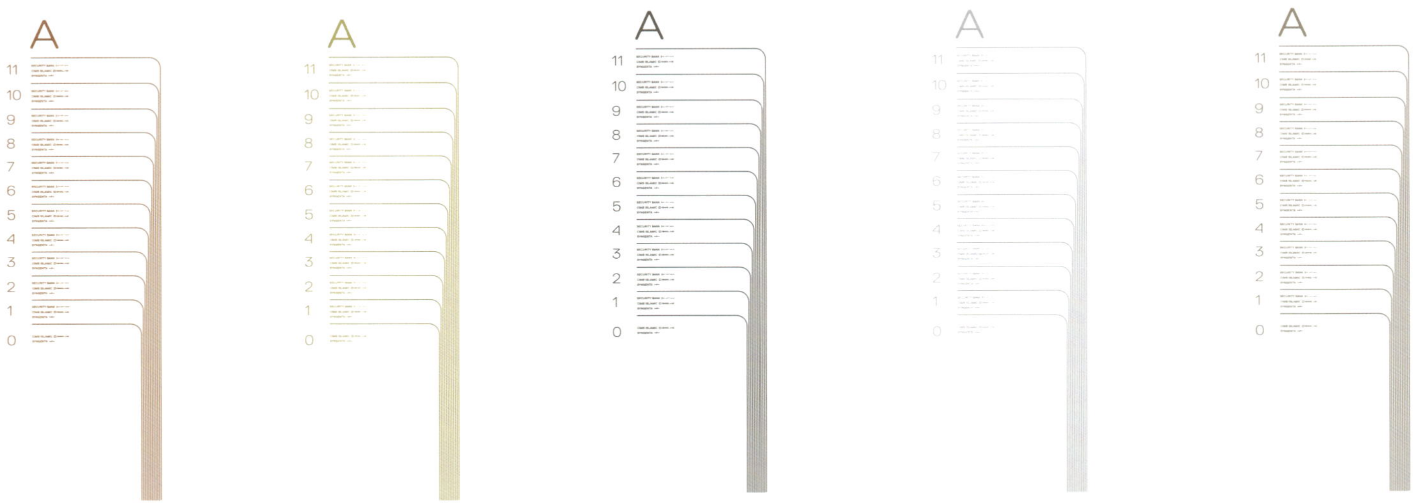
A
11
10
9
8
7
6
5
4
3
2
1
0

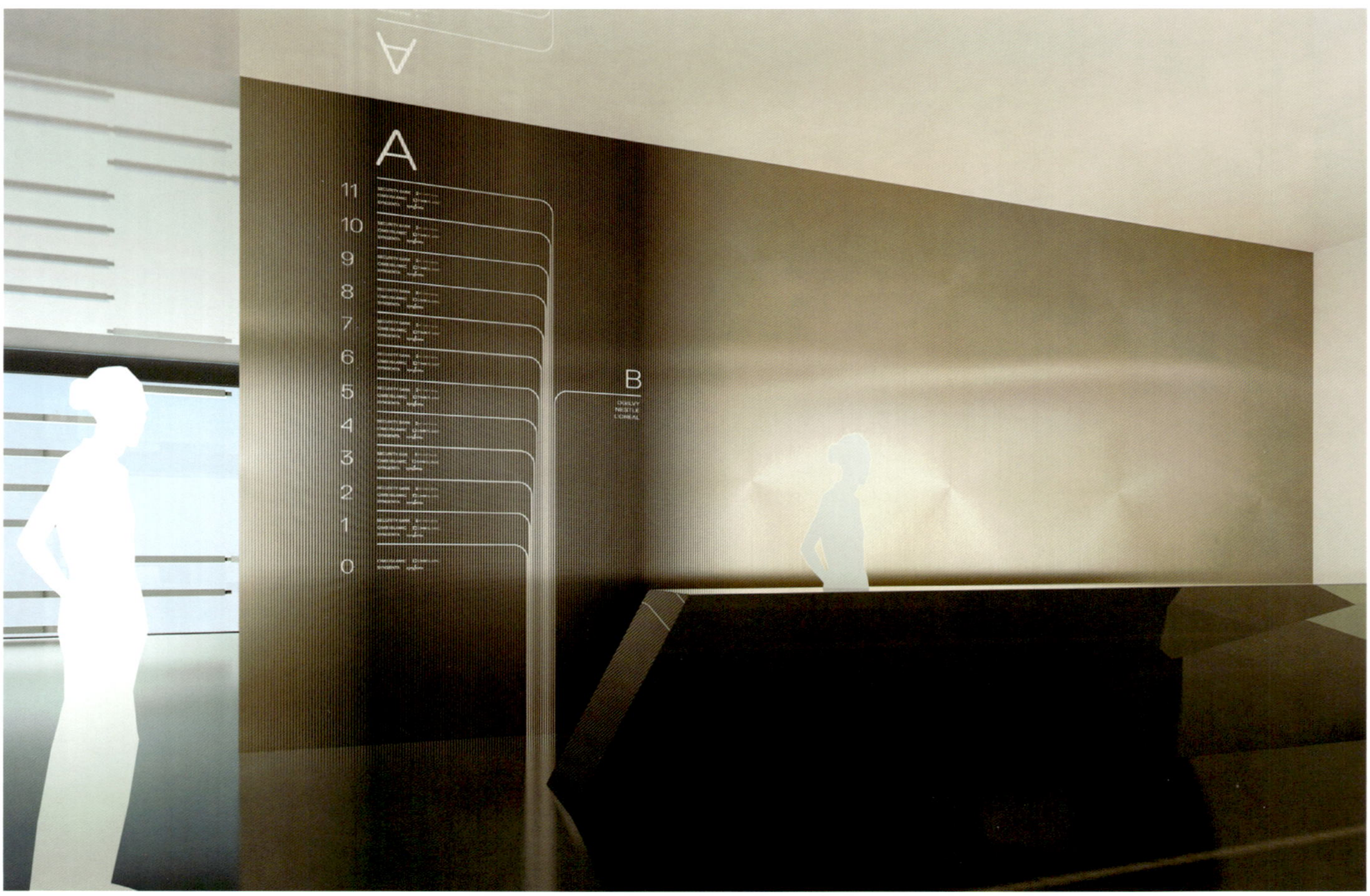
A
11
10
9
8
7
6
5
4
3
2
1
0
B

SILVER

To the North of Silver Retail Core

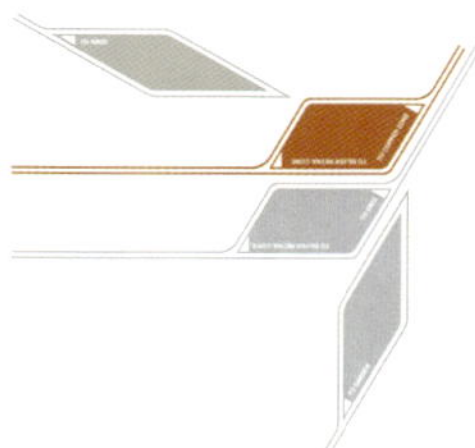

COPPER

To the North of Copper Retail Core

BRONZE

To the North of Bronze Retail Core

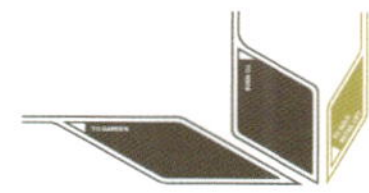

GOLD

To the North of Gold Retail Core

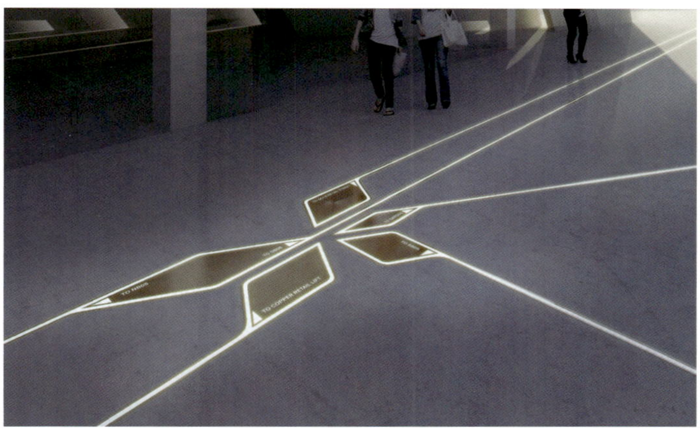

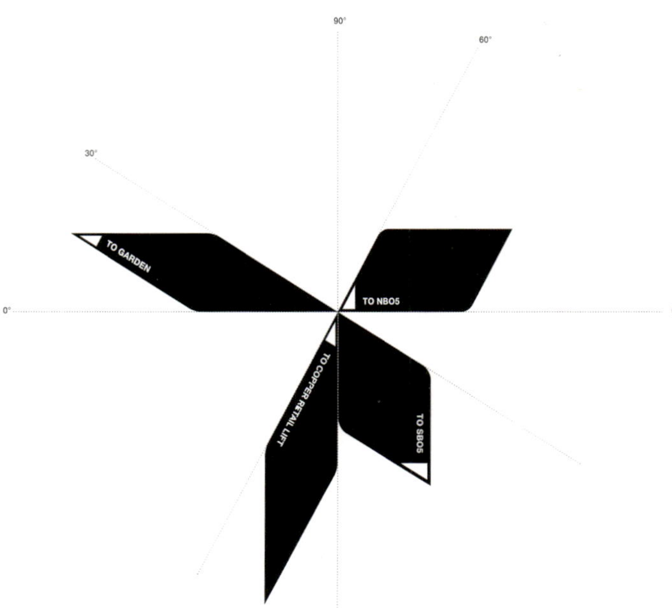

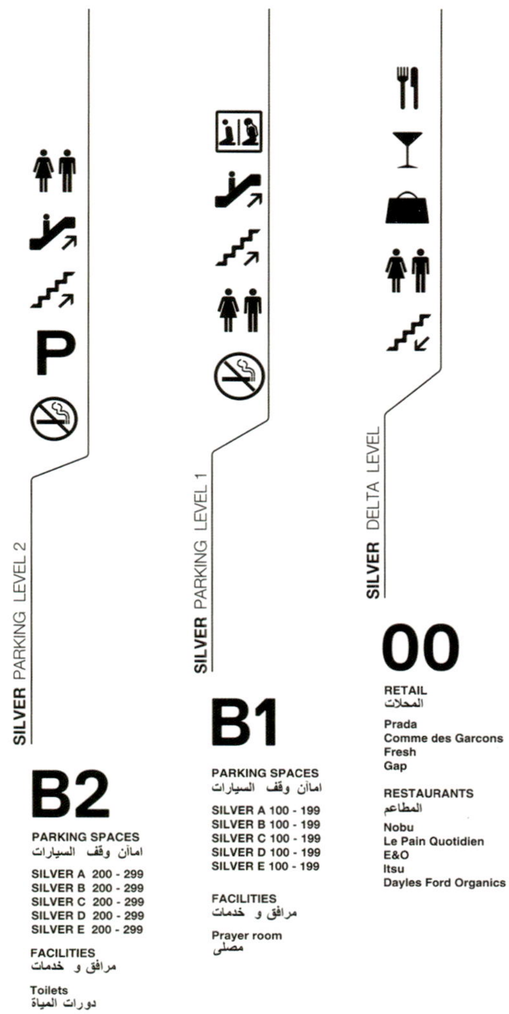

Videotron's Flagship Store

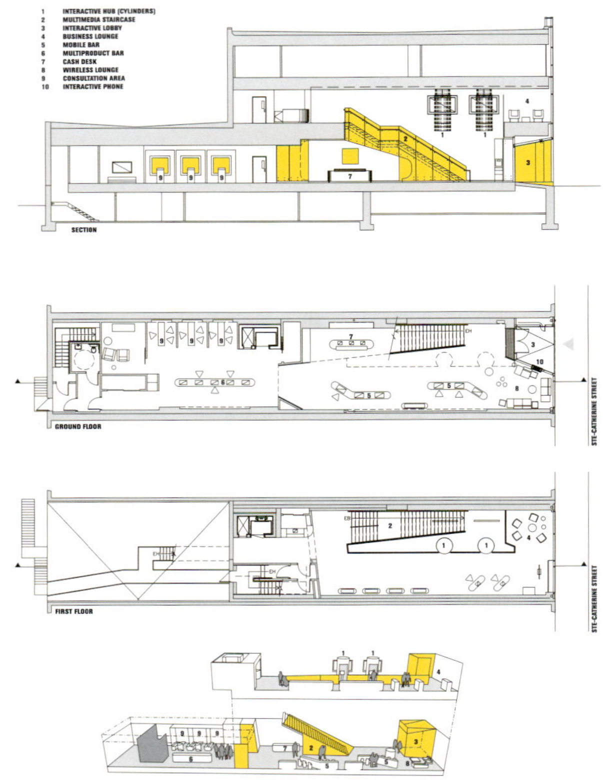

This avant-garde business complex in downtown Montreal has an instore environment that offers a new customer experience. Melded with the dazzling multimedia interior design, the signage system and store decor bring the brand to life with new interactive ways of showcasing the products in this highly competitive sector.

Designer: Sid Lee **Client:** Videotron **Location:** Montreal, Canada

VIDÉOTRON
Une compagnie de Quebecor Media
ÉTUDIANTS, RÉPONDEZ
NOUVEAU FORFAIT
EXCLUSIF AUX ÉTUDIANTS
EXCEPTIONNELLEMENT
24 95 $
1192
SAMSUNG

2e
SERVICE Affaires
ZONE illico
Service
1er
ZONE Mobile

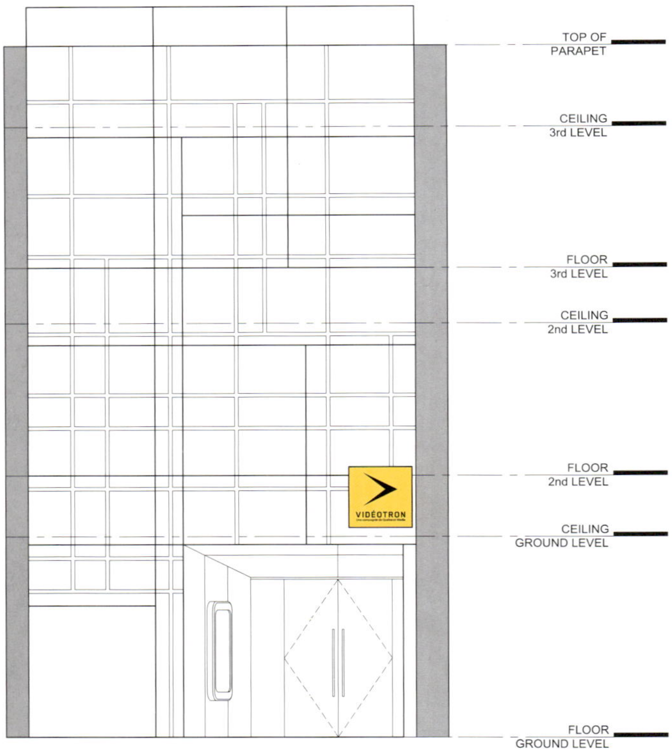
TOP OF
PARAPET
CEILING
3rd LEVEL
FLOOR
3rd LEVEL
CEILING
2nd LEVEL
FLOOR
2nd LEVEL
CEILING
GROUND LEVEL
FLOOR
GROUND LEVEL
VIDÉOTRON

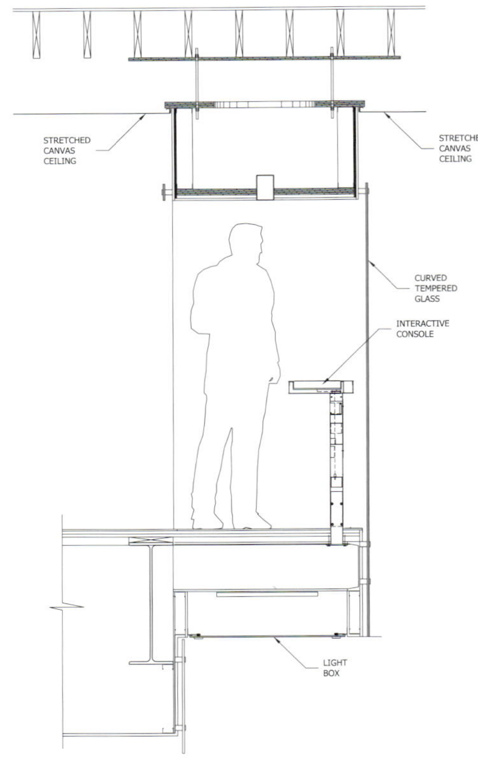
STRETCHED
CANVAS
CEILING
STRETCHED
CANVAS
CEILING
CURVED
TEMPERED
GLASS
INTERACTIVE
CONSOLE
LIGHT
BOX

2e
SERVICE
Affaires
ZONE
illico
Service
1er
ZONE
Mobile
ZONE
ZONE
Multiproduit

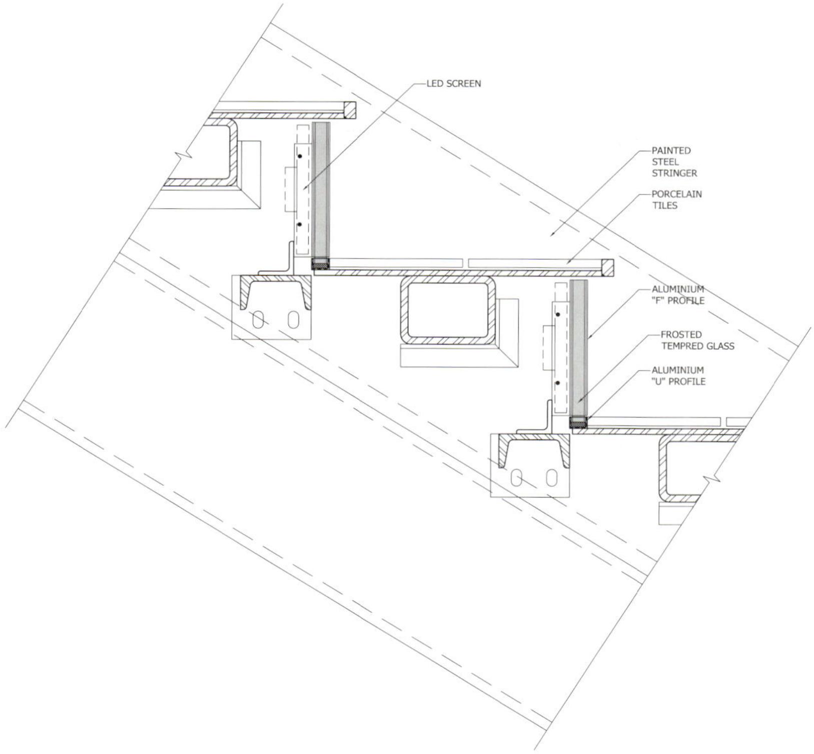
LED SCREEN
PAINTED STEEL STRINGER
PORCELAIN TILES
ALUMINIUM "F" PROFILE
FROSTED TEMPRED GLASS
ALUMINIUM "U" PROFILE

2e
SERVICE Affaires
ZONE illico
Service
1er
ZONE Mobile
ZONE Télé nume
ZONE Multiprod
ZONE Multiproduit
BEAUX ET INTELLIGENTS.

Vienna Airport

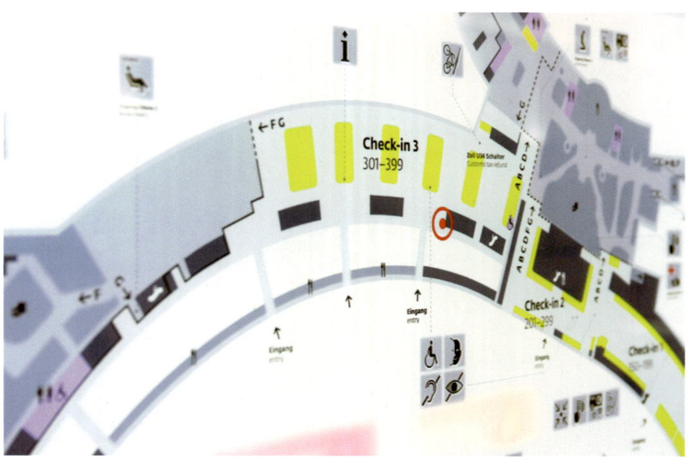

Signs in this newly extended airport are characterized by pure design in an understated, legible, poetic way. Clean typeface is chosen with graduating colours. The glass media shifts from translucent to transparent in a vertical plane. Vivid pictograms and scenographic effects produced by transparency, shadow and light have brightened the signage appearance while fully complying with the legibility requirements for passengers on the move. In this public facility, the signage system helps to establish a serene, visually friendly and comfortable environment.

Design Firm: Intégral Ruedi Baur Paris & Zurich **Designer:** Ruedi Baur, Eva Kubinyi, Simon Burkart, Christina Poth, Axel Steinberger, Wanja Ledowski, Maria Roszkowska, Gabriela Wolfertz, David Esser **Photographer:** Andras Körner **Client:** Vienna Airport **Location:** Vienna, Austria

ABCD
willkommen in Wien
tervetuloa Wieniin
velkommen til Wien
velkommen til Wien
bienvenue à Vienne
esiet sveicināti Vīne
Добре дошли във Виена
ウィーンへようこそ
välkommen till Wien
dobrodošli u Beč
velkomin í Vín
witamy w Wiedniu
welcome to Vienna
viyana'ya Hoş Geldiniz
benvenuti a Vienna
vítejte ve Vídni
sveiki atvykę į Vieną
bienvenidos a Viena
hartelijk welkom in Wenen
isten hozta Bécsben
dobrodošli na Dunaju
Καλώς ορίσατε στην Βιένη
欢迎来到维也纳

10
09
08
07
06

F33
G31
F25
G27
F27

The Citypark Shopping Mall

The signage system for this shopping mall is based on the dynamic presentation of primary colors and the minimalist design concept. With saturated red and blue, the pictograms stem from the redesign of an old logo. The outdoor signage uses the same intense color scheme to make the building stand out in the surrounding areas and promote the shopping mall's visual identity. Integrated into the artistic interior wall graphics, the signage system adds a creative and modern flavor to this mall, creating a compelling and entertaining shopping environment.

Design Firm: Studio 360 **Designer:** Vladan Srdic **Photographer:** Studio 360 **Client:** McCann **Location:** Ljubljana, Slovenia

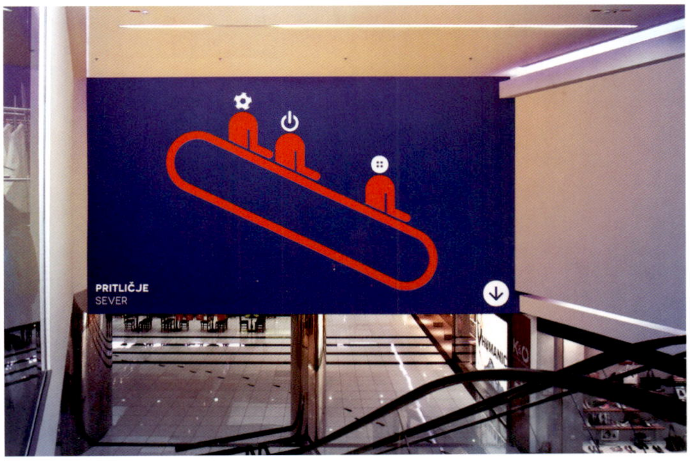
PRITLIČJE
SEVER

PARKIRNA HIŠA
VHOD
DOBRODOŠLI
PON. - NED.
06H - 23H
P
city park
3.ETAŽA
2.ETAŽA
1.ETAŽA
PRITLIČJE
355
356
355
356

APPETITE
RD.
25M
1
GOSSIP
ST.
30M
0

The Cathay Carpark

Design Firm: Manic Design **Designer:** Karen Huang, Adeline Chong, Benjamin Koh, Wong Chee Yi **Photographer:** John Nursalim **Client:** Cathay Organization **Location:** Singapore

In this carpark which belongs to a cinema and a shopping mall, two out of six floors don't have direct access to the shopping mall. In order to solve this wayfinding problem, the design team adopted different wall colors to decorate different levels, and placed the floor information in large bold font on the featured walls, stairwells and doors of each floor. Coupled with LED sign boxes hanging from the ceiling, this signage system clearly guides users to the correct location.

TO SHOPS &
ALL CARPARK
LEVELS

EXIT
SHOPS
THROUGH
CARPARK
4

↑ 2M
2
↓ 1M

SHOPS
NO ENTRY
EXIT
SLOW
GIVE WAY
NO ACCESS
TO SHOPS
2

MORE LOTS
SHOPS
EXIT
WAY
OUT

BSL Garage House

This wayfinding project strives to deliver an effective signage solution for an old public garage. The directional signs were divided into two groups to individually serve pedestrians and vehicles. The designer used LED diodes beneath some signs for better visibility on a gray surface. Pictograms on the wall are incorporated with roundels to enliven the atmosphere. With bright colors highlighting the backgrounds and causing a stunning visual effect, this wayfinding system readily assists people and creates a more pleasant, friendly public space.

Design Firm: Studio 360 **Designer:** Vladan Srdic **Photographer:** Studio 360 **Client:** BSL d.o.o. **Location:** Ljubljana, Slovenia

GARAGE
PROSTO
ODPRTO 24 UR

SREČNO POT
SAFE JOURNEY
GUTE REISE
BUON VIAGGIO
BON VO

BLAGAJNA / PAY TO PARK
IZHOD / EXIT

8

BLAGAJNA

Car Dealer Pappas

Design Firm: büro uebele visuelle kommunikation **Designer:** Beate Kapprell, Andreas Uebele **Architect:** kadawittfeldarchitektur **Photographer:** Andreas Körner
Client: Pappas Group **Location:** Salzburg, Austria

Pappas' signage system guides vehicles through the dealership's drive-through indoor structure. Destinations and other information appear in large black letters on white crash barriers with arrows: Car wash, Car park, Service and Sales. The familiar barriers effectively guide car owners. This signage design caters to the open architectural structure and presents characteristics of a professional car dealership.

INFORMATION VERKAUF

AUSFAHRT

SERVICE
SERVICE

MITARBEITER
LEHRWERKSTATT
BETRIEBSARZT

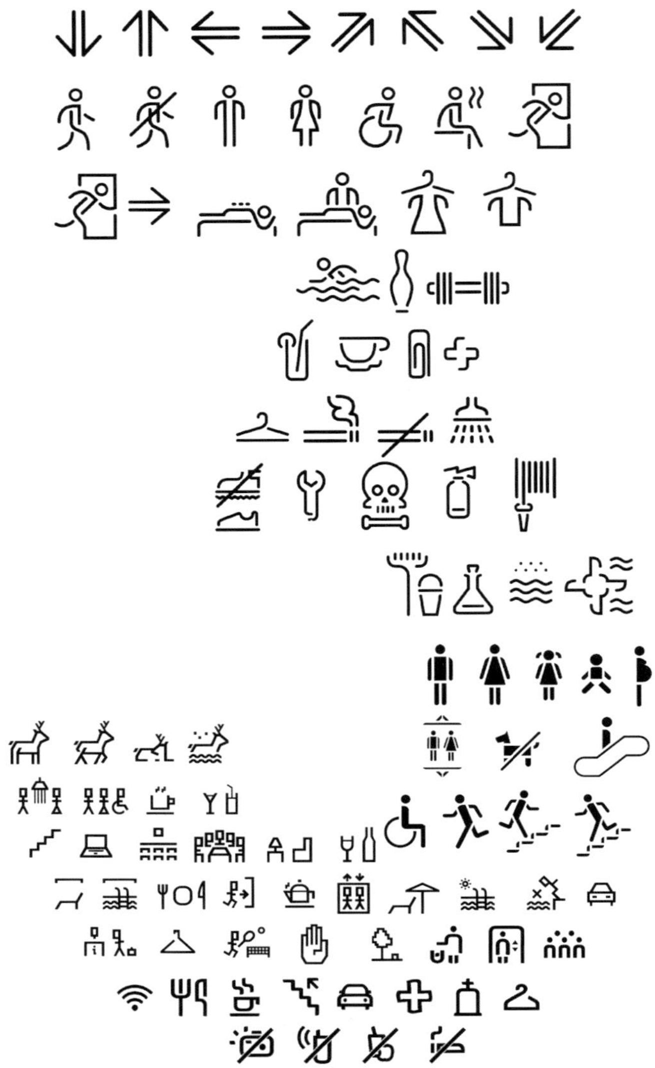

BUSINESS CENTERS

Wayfinding in Business Centers: Brand Your Offices

Providing guidance is always the most basic task of signage systems. Because time and efficiency are priorities in the office space, time available to find your way around is very limited. A signage system in offices, therefore, can not fail this fundamental assignment. A neat and clean sign design is usually appreciated within a corporation, since unnecessary elements disturb and confuse people, wasting their valuable time. Directional cues in a business center are also expected to be easily remembered and legible, with familiar illustrations and unambiguous information.

A recognizable brand design will increase a business's popularity and stimulate a high demand for their product. The signage system is precisely the tool to further promote the brand image. By referring to the brand logo and adopting a cohesive icon system, or using large graphics that demonstrate corporate culture and history, the signage systems evolve from merely functional signs to an effective advertising medium. It visualizes the corporate culture in the corridors, lift, lobbies and on every door, relentlessly hinting at the brand personality and shaping the office spaces.

Vivid and refreshing signage projects impress clients at first sight, infusing their wayfinding experiences with implicit promotion of brand identity. These projects also unceasingly remind employees of the corporate culture, creating a distinct work space for them that promotes for the job.

Google Engineering Headquarters

Google, world-leading technology company, created an entertaining and ingenious engineering headquarters. The office was built into a whimsical space with computer workstations and game rooms. The decoration and signage exhibit diverse themes; names of game rooms adopt the typical typefaces in corresponding games; important signs are shown on conspicuous places near switch boards. To guide the staff, signage is painted on the ground of corridors where signage is demonstrated upon a black track.

This synchronization of wayfinding system and interior decoration transforms a regular office center into a visionary and sparkling home of novel ideas.

Design Firm: Pension design **Designer:** Lee Pension **Photographer:** David Barbour **Client:** Google **Location:** Westminster, London

DIRECTOR
FP 09
FP 08
FP 07
FP 12
FP 11
FP 10
MK
GOOGLE FIELDS
PRINT
TECH STOP
STORE
24 VC
ROUTE-MASTER BUS
BUS LANE
LIFT LOBBY
MEETING ROOMS
12 VC
POST ROOM/ XRAY
EXISTING IDF ROOM 1
EXISTING UPS
UNISEX SHOWERS
DELI PREP KITCHEN
PLANT
DELI
FP 06
FP 05
FP 04
FP 03
FP 02
FP 01
FIRST AID
MASSAGE ROOM
Network Operations Huddle

FROGGER
360

CENTIPEDE
CENTIPEDE
375

DEFENDER
NOTICE
THIS AREA

L3

NOTICE
THIS AREA

CAUTION
INFLAMMABLE

QUADRANT 1

Q2
Q2
ROOMS
VINT CERF
EDSGER DIJKSTRA
ANDREW S. TANENBAUM
ALAN TURING
DONALD KNUTH
CHARLES BABBAGE
JOHN VON NEUMANN
JIM GRAY
KURT GÖDEL
WHITFIELD DIFFIE
TECH STOP
RINT AREA 1
THE COG
KITCHEN
ONLY

EDP Porto

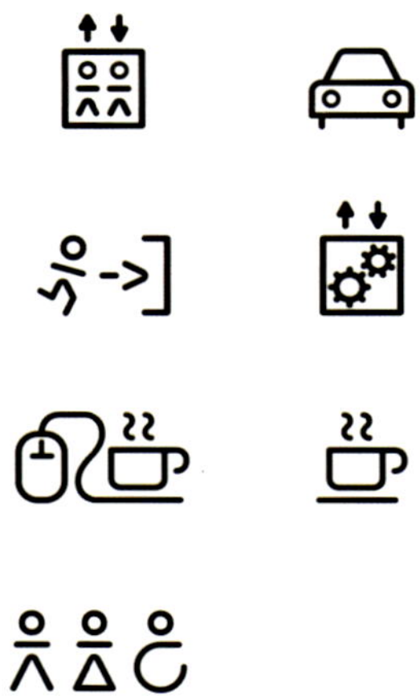

This signage system borrowed the exclusive typeface used in the energy supplier's earlier identity project. This mellow font is applied in all text signs in straightforward black and white. Pictographs are also inspired by the font, adopting soft geometric lines to form different images. This signage is a clean and effective design that consistently presents elements of a specific typeface, clearly leading the visitors to their desired destination. With the brand identity integrated in the signage, a more distinct business place is built.

Design Firm: R2 **Art & Creative Direction:** Lizá Ramalho and Artur Rebelo **Design:** Lizá Ramalho and Artur Rebelo, assisted by Artur Faria **Photographer:** Filipe Braga **Client:** Fundação EDP — Porto **Location:** Porto, Portugal

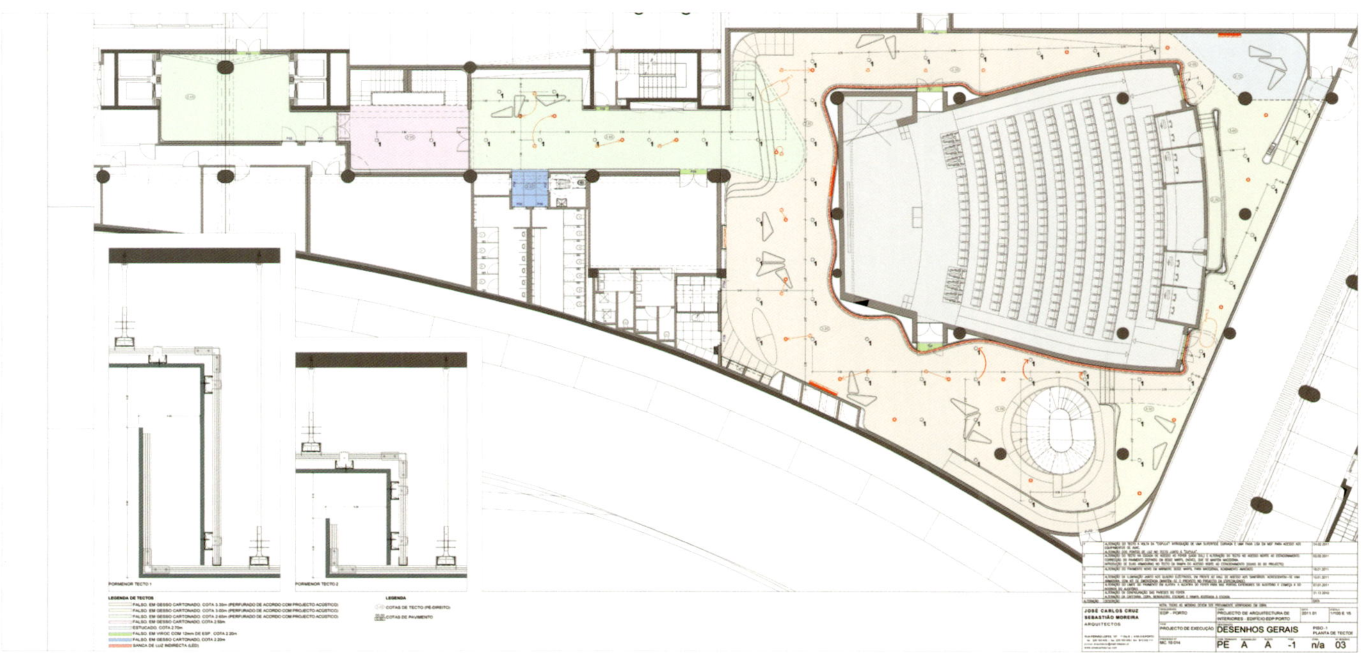
JOSÉ CARLOS CRUZ
SEBASTIÃO MOREIRA
ARQUITECTOS
EDP - PORTO
PROJECTO DE ARQUITECTURA DE INTERIORES - EDIFÍCIO EDP PORTO
PROJECTO DE EXECUÇÃO
DESENHOS GERAIS
PISO -1
PLANTA DE TECTOS
PE A A -1 n/a 03

Centro de Reuniões
Cafetaria
WC
Receção

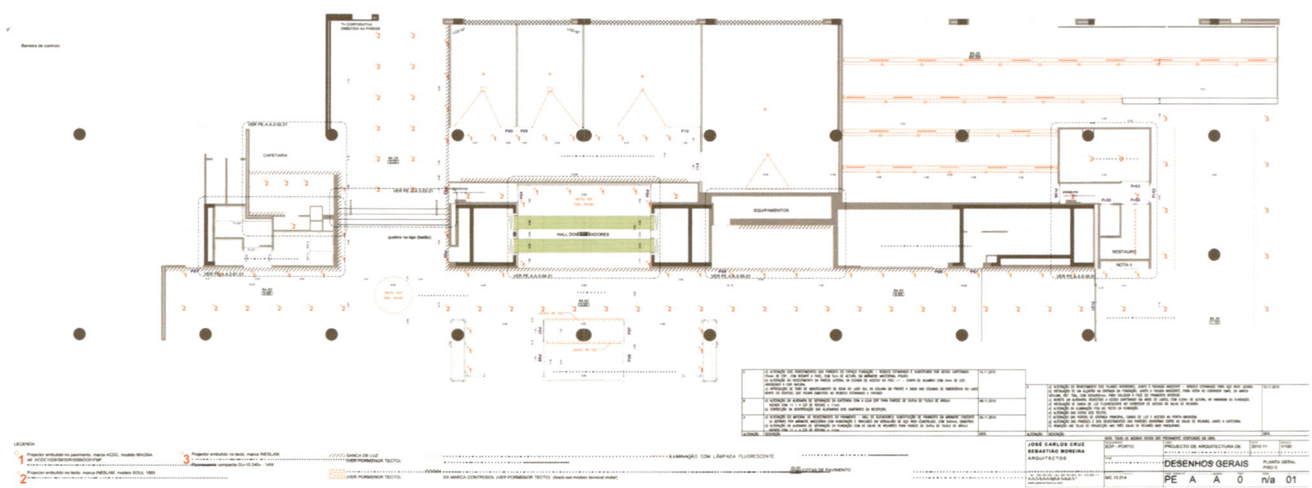
JOSÉ CARLOS CRUZ
SEBASTIÃO MOREIRA
ARQUITECTOS
DESENHOS GERAIS
PE A A 0 n/a 01

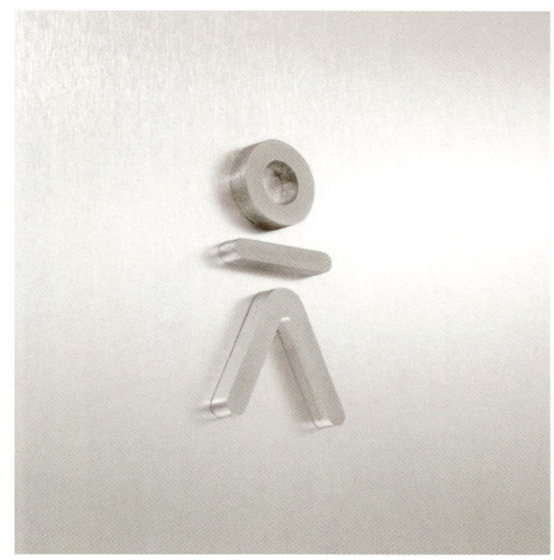

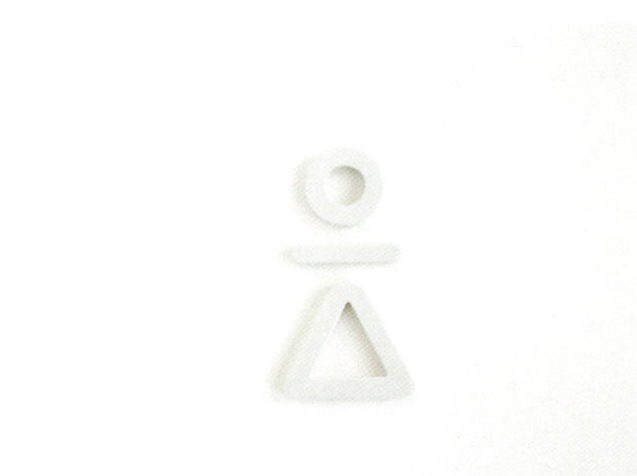

Office "Publicus"

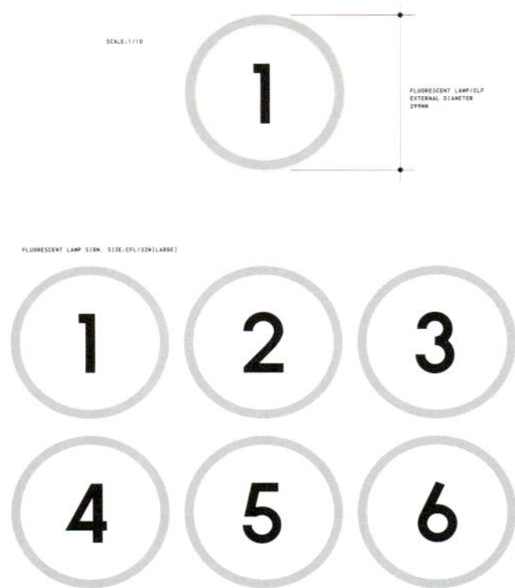

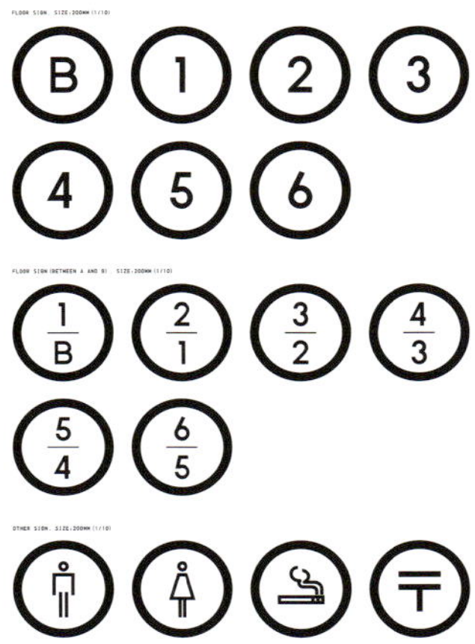

The office building has an identity of a circle emitting light with a diameter of 2 meters. This logo is adopted to represent various aspects of the space. The level number is integrated within a luminous circle, highlighting the information and working in concert with the office's branding.

Design Firm: Nosigner **Designer:** Isuke Tachikawa **Location:** Japan

3

4

Grauforz Steel

The signage promotes brand awareness, as the same colour is used in the brand logo. Huge red numbers on transparent glass walls make it easy to find the appropriate office.

Design Firm: Anagrama **Designer:** Anagrama **Photographer:** Caroga Photographer **Client:** Grauforz Steel **Location:** Monterrey, Mexico

Sistemas
IT SERVICES

Vice-Presidencia
Servicios Compartidos
SHARED SERVICES VICE-PRESIDENT

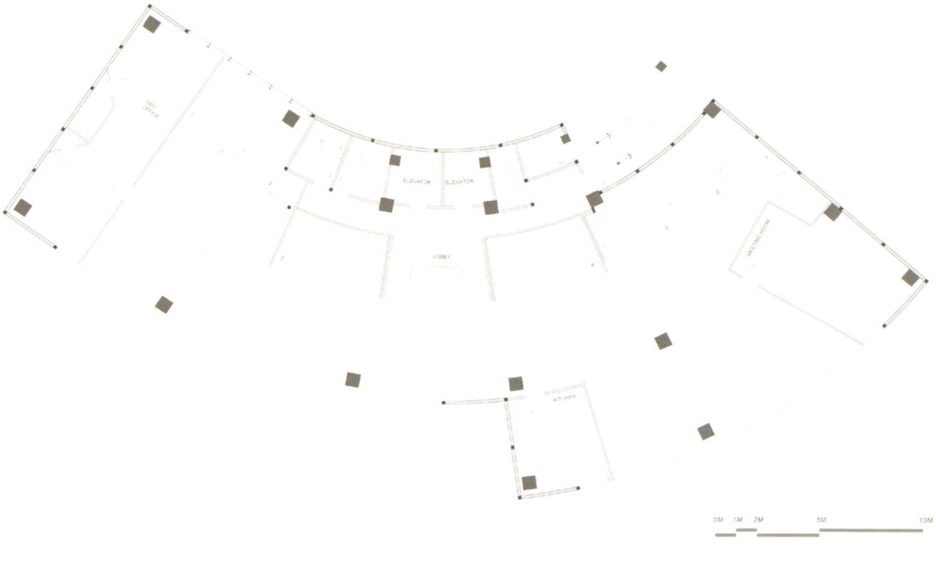

The "Journey to Parramatta"

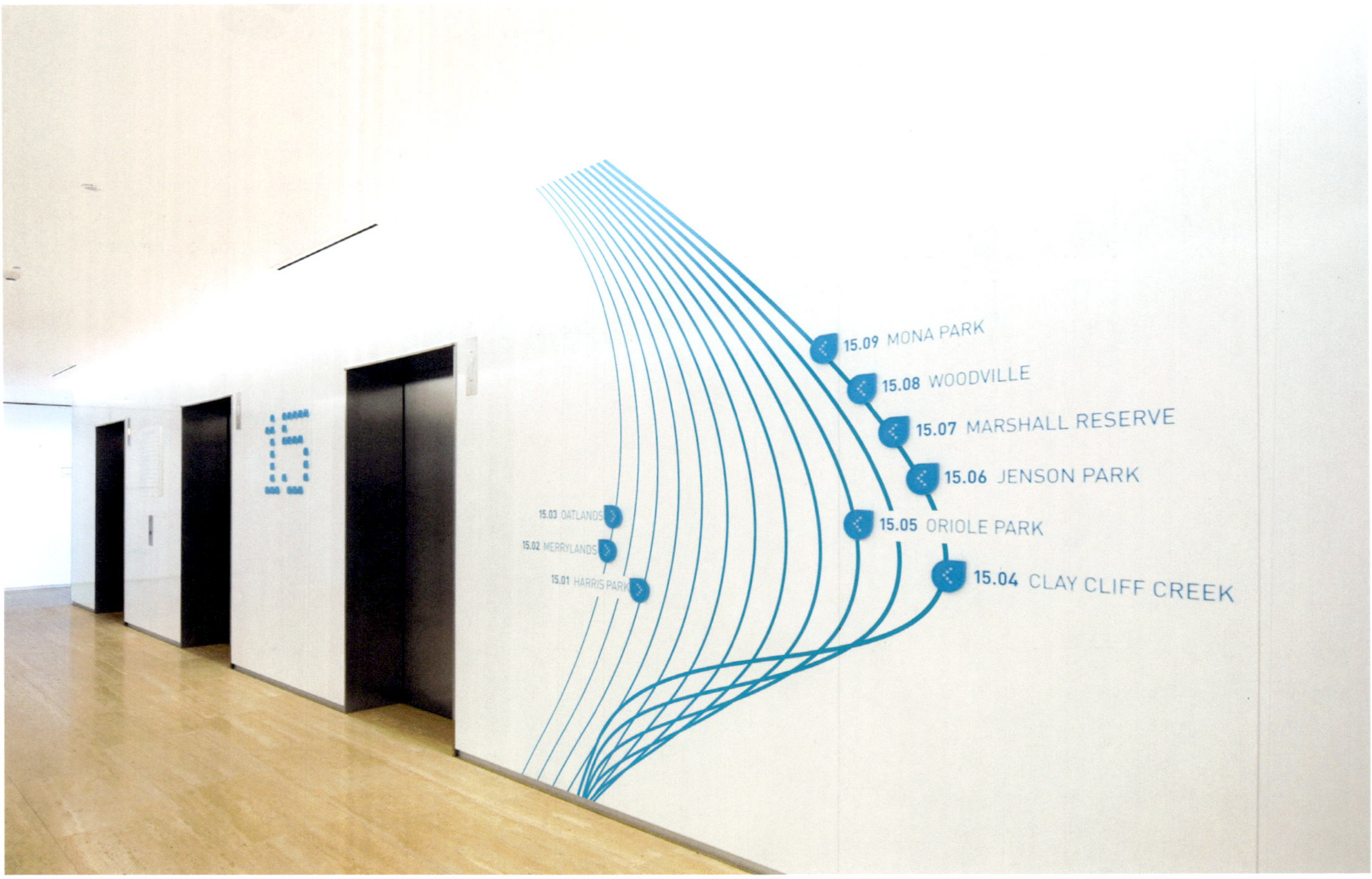

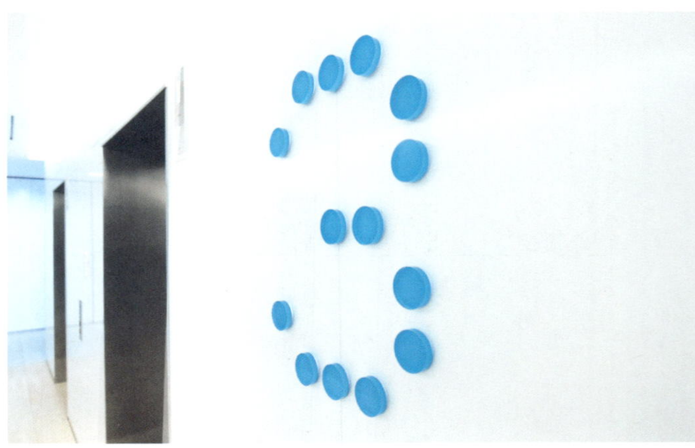

Design Firm: BrandCulture Communications Pty Ltd **Designer:** Stephen Minning, Antonijo Bacic, David Ing **Photographer:** Philip Poyner **Client:** Sydney Water
Location: Sydney, Australia

Sydney Water, Parramatta - Lift Directory

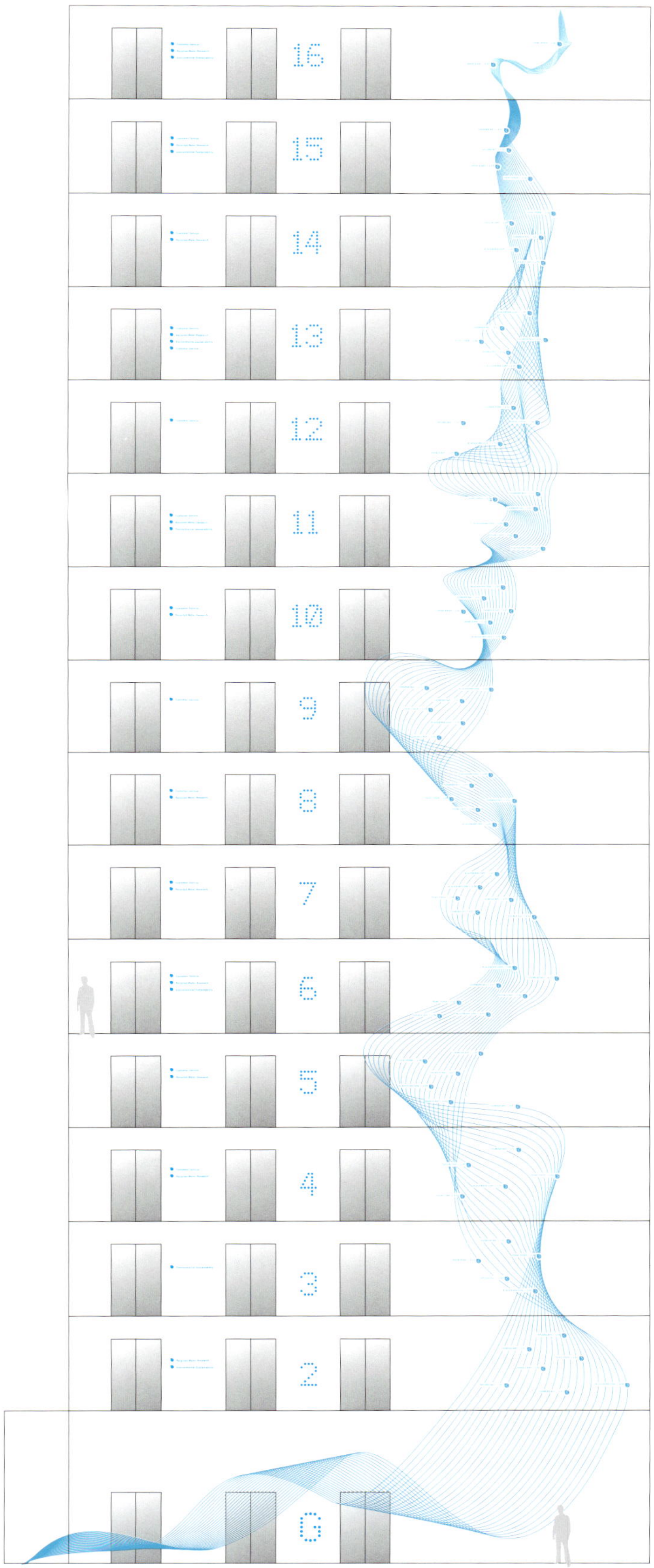

Sydney Water is a water service corporation with a profound history. Its wayfinding and graphics package named "Journey to Parramatta" reflects the culture and story of Sydney Water.

The core of the idea is the creation of a graphic of the Parramatta river, providing a visual narrative of Sydney Water's history. The graphic spreads inside the building from the ground floor, where the journey begins in Sydney Harbor, to the top floor. Each lift lobby features a graphic representation of the river sections, listing the meeting rooms with their corresponding stories for easy navigation. Large numbers made from laser-cut acrylic adorn the walls of the lobbies, sitting 10mm off the wall to create a floating effect as on the water.

This novel and poetic design infuses this office building with a quiet flow of history. It innovatively and effectively unfolds information, elegantly demonstrating Sydney Water's heritage, and its constant social responsibilities to the city.

9
10
11
11.01 Homebush Bay
11.02 Meadowbank
11.03 Brays Bay
11.04 Rhodes Park
11.05 Powells Creek
11.06 Liberty Grove
11.07 West Ryde
11.08 Concord West
11.09 Strathfield
11.10 Eastwood
12
12.01 George Kendall Reserve
12.02 Melrose Park
12.03 Alrey Park
12.04 Bressignton Park
12.05 Boronia Park
12.06 Sumerville Park
12.07 Dence Park
13.01
13.02
13.03
13.04
13.05
13.06
13.07
13.08
13.09
13.10

KF-824

Parramatta Park
The indigenous inhabitants were the Burramatta ('burra' meaning eel and 'matta' meaning creek) clan of the Dharug people. In 1788 Governor Phillip chose Parramatta Park as the second settlement of New South Wales.

Edelweiss House

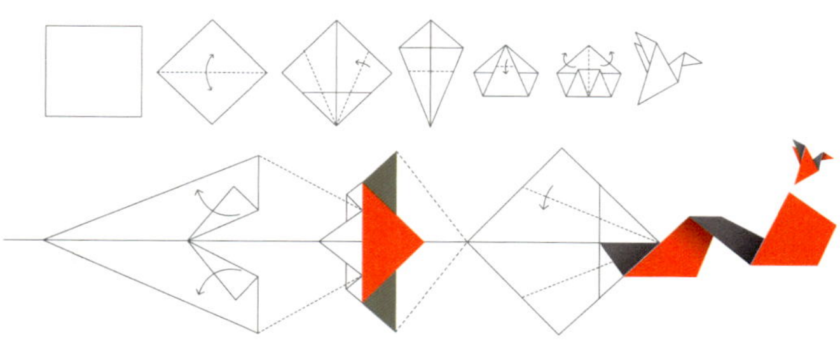

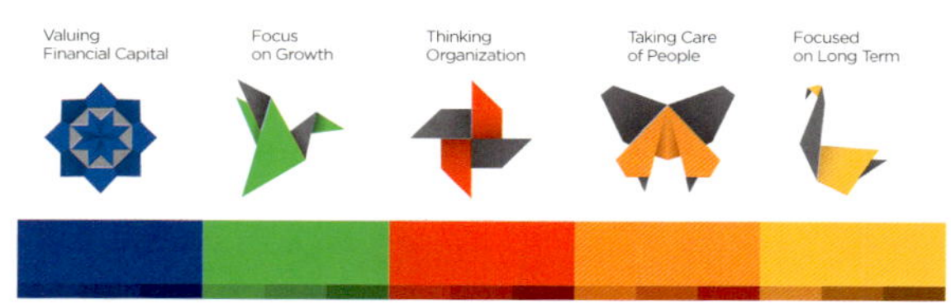

The signage and graphic design for financial institution Edelweiss is inspired by Japanese origami to depict the expertise of the financial powerhouse. A typeface reflecting the art of folding was developed and further executed as floor identification signs on each floor, strengthening the idea of crafting. Material and fixture processes were carefully selected to devise a flexible system for changing identification signs as required as the parking basements at Edelweiss are cold and dark without sunlight, vivid orange, green and yellow wayfinding signs were chosen to create a cheerful environment in sync with the entire building.

The innovative forms of the signage system resonate with the principles, open mindedness, transparency and efficiency across floors. This wayfinding design expresses both sophistication and the endlessly inventive spirit of the company.

Design Firm: Leaf Design Pvt. Ltd **Photographer:** Leaf Design Pvt. Ltd **Client:** Edelweiss House **Location:** Mumbai, India

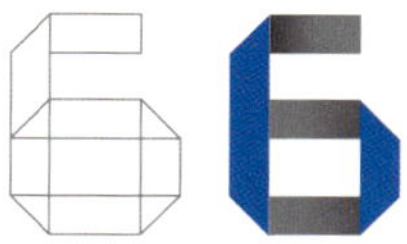

G1234567890

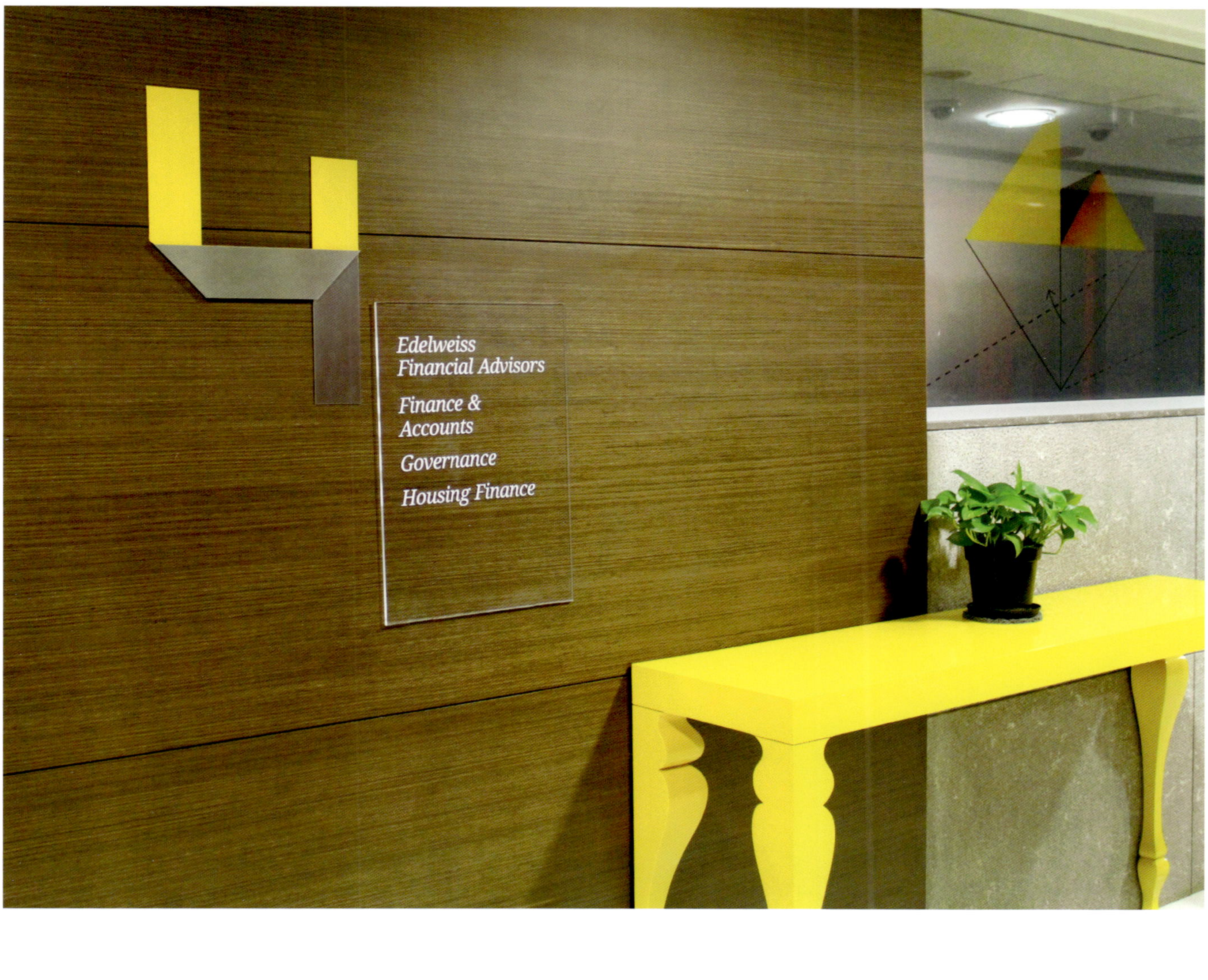

Airship

Men

6
North

15
South

B2
B2

Zetland House

The new signs for the warehouse-style office Zetland were inspired by nearly extinct hand-printed advertising signage in the neighborhood. In a nostalgic manner, original designs were drawn by hand and applied directly to the walls from external signposts to internal route indicators. Monochrome texts are legible, and reveal modern simplicity. This signage design reflects the individual characteristics of a warehouse-style office.

Design Firm: Bunch **Designer:** Denis Kovac **Photographer:** ©Bunch **Client:** Zetland House **Location:** London

ZETLAND HOUSE
5—25 SCRUTTON STREET
ZETLANDHOUSE.COM
LOWER GROUND
THE VAULT GYM
SIGNAL GALLERY
THE VAULT GYM
CAFÉ Z
PORTLAND APARTMENTS
7DIGITAL
PAPER MACHE TIGER
GROUND
SHUTL
MYLAKO
MINNOW FILMS
BLACKBRIDGE COMMUNICATIONS
VYRE
VYRE
VYRE
FIRST
IMAGE LINE COMMUNICATIONS
EMPOWERING LEARNING
JACOB BAILEY
SPINACH BANKSTHOMAS
ALMEIDA CAPITAL
MAXXIMA LABMED IML SWIM
THE LATE NIGHT SALON
STYLESIGHT
SECOND
EMPEROR
EMPEROR
EMPEROR
WAY TO BLUE
BOSSA STUDIOS
IOGEN
IOGEN
THIRD
TOWNSHEND LANDSCAPE
ARCHITECTS
PLUCK UK / DEMAND MEDIA
OPTIMITY
POWSTER
SPOTLESS INTERACTIVE
AVANTI CONSULTING
THIRD
DRAGONFLY FILM & TV
ASITE
TYRRELL KATZ
BEAUTIFUL WORLD
EGELNICK AND WEBB
EGELNICK AND WEBB
FOURTH
AUGUST
AUGUST
AUGUST
AUGUST
SOMESUCH & CO
CAFÉDIRECT
CAFÉDIRECT
BLOCK H
RHAPSODY
SKILLED CAREERS
CHALAYAN
SQUIZ

LIFT THREE
LIFT
3

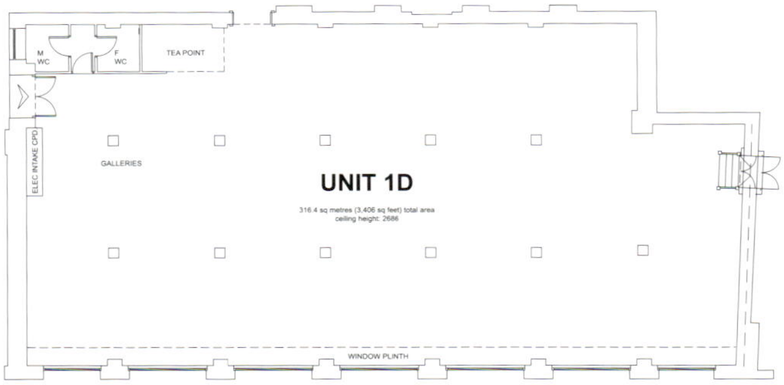
M WC
F WC
TEA POINT
ELEC INTAKE CPD
GALLERIES
UNIT 1D
316.4 sq metres (3,406 sq feet) total area
ceiling height: 2686
WINDOW PLINTH

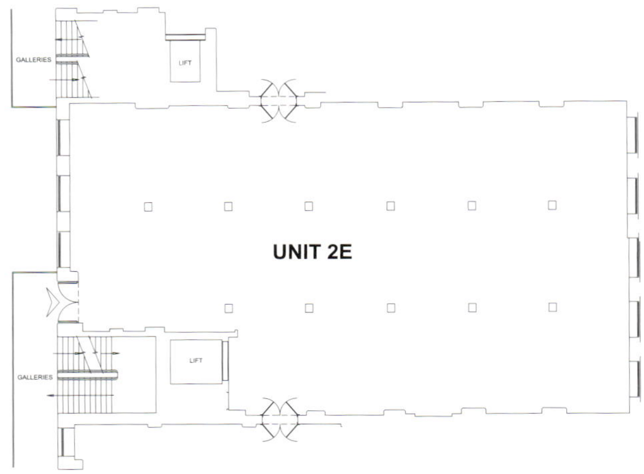
GALLERIES
LIFT
UNIT 2E
LIFT
GALLERIES

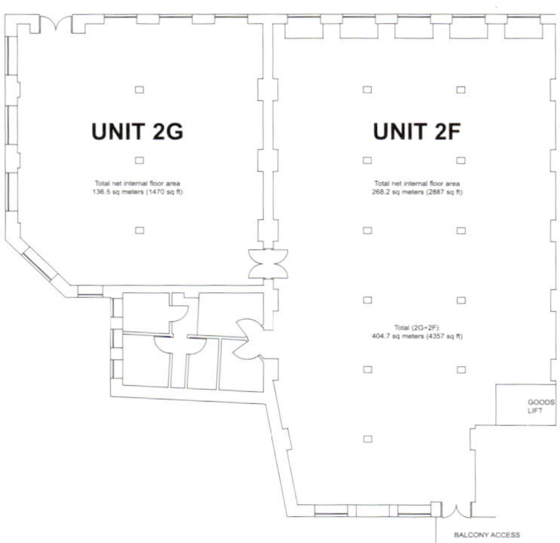
UNIT 2G
Total net internal floor area
136.5 sq meters (1470 sq ft)
UNIT 2F
Total net internal floor area
268.2 sq meters (2887 sq ft)
Total (2G+2F):
404.7 sq meters (4357 sq ft)
GOODS LIFT
BALCONY ACCESS

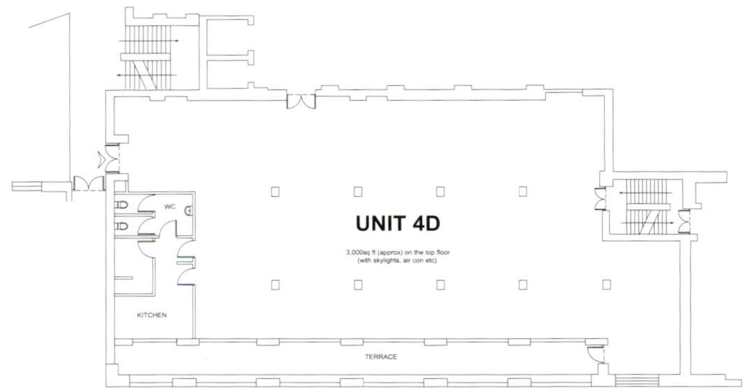
WC
UNIT 4D
3,000sq ft (approx) on the top floor
(with skylights, air con etc)
KITCHEN
TERRACE

LIFT
1

LOWER
GROUND FLOOR
UNITS A&B

MEETING
ROOM
Z2

LIFT TWO
LIFT
2

Alta Diagonal

The starting point for this project sprang from the name, and was based the building's location in Barcelona. This neighbourhood is popularly known as the zona alta "high-end district" in the Diagonal area.

To give the building its own personality and stress its location on Avinguda Diagonal "Diagonal Avenue", the designers made a series of diagonal cutting through the typeface. The elements in the design of the building's signage were deliberately oversized to correspond to the exact size of the pieces of cladding to create highly visible signs that fitted with the architecture. This integration continued in the same vein with the choice of material: stainless steel, a material which complemented other materials selected by the architects when redesigning the building.

Design Firm: Clase bcn **Designer:** Clase bcn **Photographer:** Clase bcn **Client:** Deka Inmobilien **Location:** Barcelona, Spain

WC
A

WC
D
C
WC

SALA DE CONFERÈNCIES
SALA DE CONFERENCIAS
CONFERENCE ROOM

Drägerwerk AG

The signage system in medical equipment manufacturer Drägerwerk AG's new building consists of hovering circles. The core of this design is an elemental, grid-style pattern of circles which differs on each storey of the building. The spacing between the circles shifts in two directions, creating gaps, clusters and distinctive formations. Codes for different rooms, levels and sections are displayed within these circles. In this way, signage is naturally incorporated on the glazed external and internal walls. The design highlights science and transparency in a medical equipment company, while contributing to the image of an innovative, secure and clear space.

Design Firm: büro uebele visuelle kommunikation **Designer:** Rebecca Benz, Katrin Theile, Katrin Dittmann, Andreas Uebele **Photographer:** Michael Heinrich **Architect:** Götz und Hootz Architekten BDA **Client:** Molvina Vermietungsgesellschaft mbH & Co. Objekt Finkenstraße KG **Location:** Lübeck, Germany

VIDEO
KONFE
RENZ
138

005–045
137–360
EBENE
3
081–108

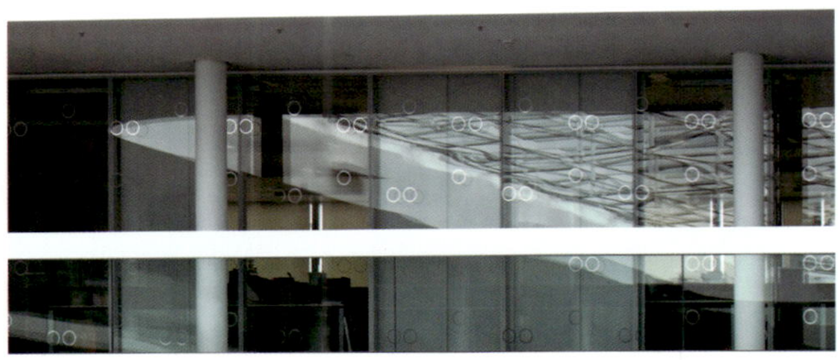

Finish Company

The black walls of classy mock-ups producer Finish act as a contrasting canvas for the company's signage system. The wayfinding information is prominently displayed in white providing clear guidance. Separate dots are used to form symbols and words. The minimalist design of symbols embodies the innovative concept of Finish and its sophisticated brand image.

Design Firm: acanforadesign **Designer:** Massimo Acanfora **Photographer:** Massimo Acanfora **Client:** Finish Creative **Location:** London

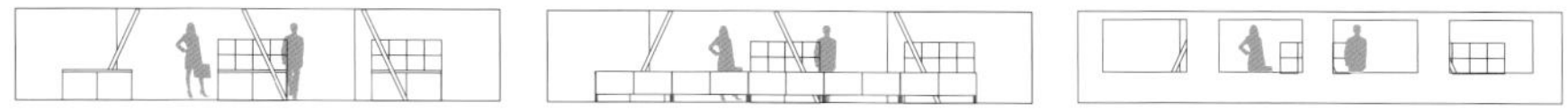

Think Tank

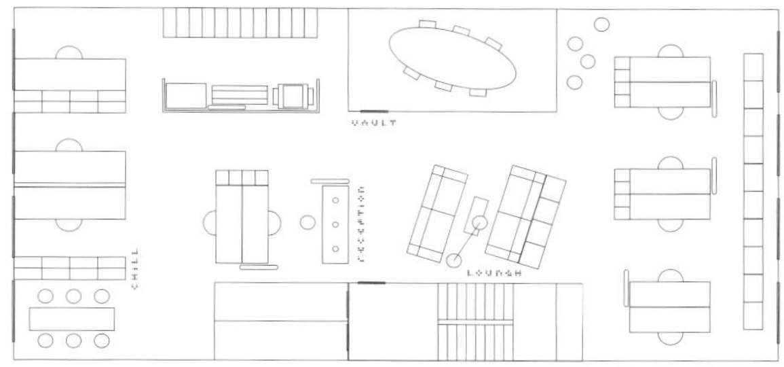

Finish:

Craft
Finish is a unique group of
who envision, develop, craft and help
for multi national
Complete Your

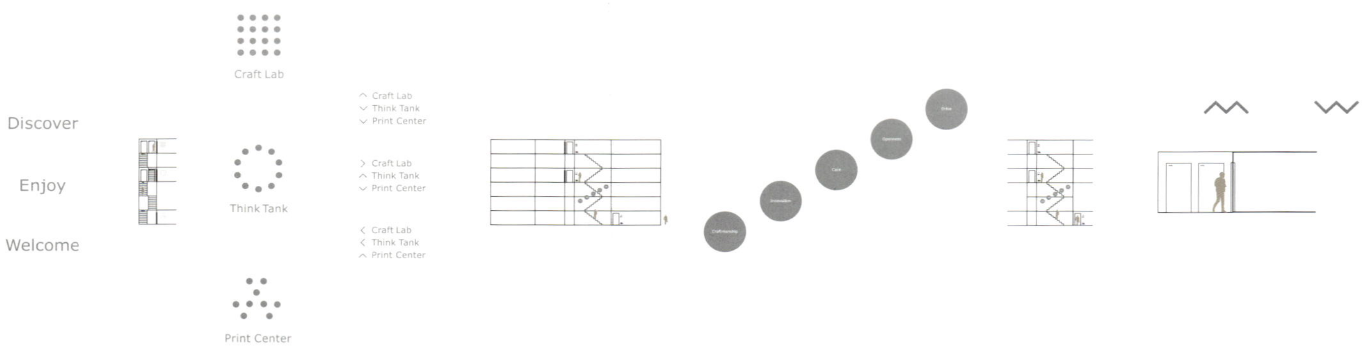
Discover
Enjoy
Welcome
Craft Lab
Think Tank
Print Center
Craft Lab
Think Tank
Print Center
Craft Lab
Think Tank
Print Center
Craft Lab
Think Tank
Print Center

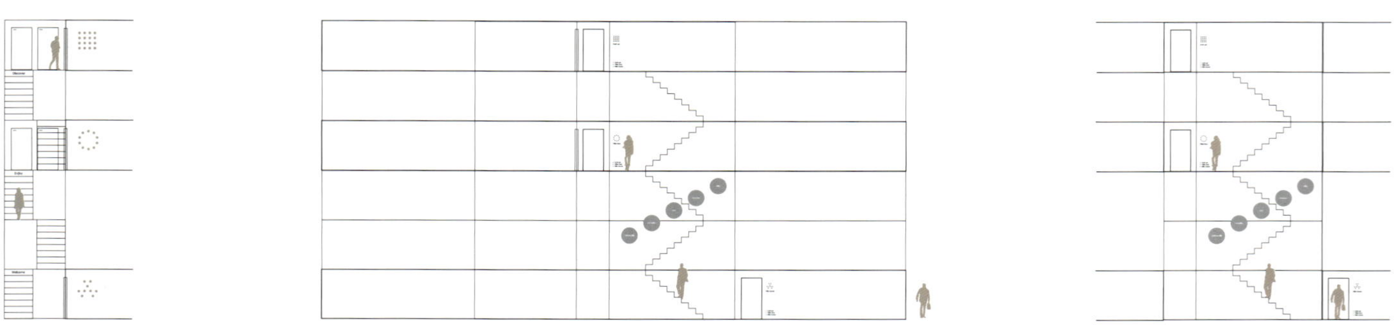

Finish:

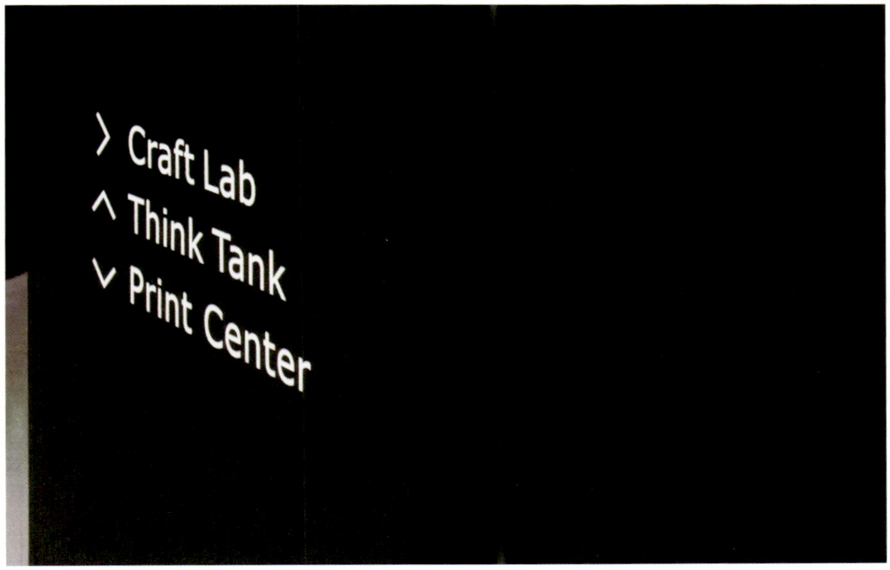
> Craft Lab
^ Think Tank
v Print Center

Think Tank
> Craft Lab
^ Think Tank
v Print Center

Mendes Júnior

The red rhombic diamond brand of this construction firm inspired the design of its signage system. The wayfinding uses red, white and black colors to establish effective instructions. Red arrows denote directions and numbers; white texts are easily legible on black backgrounds. The integration of this signage system and the woody interior decoration convey brand images of modesty and trustworthiness.

Design Firm: Greco Design **Designer:** Gustavo Greco, Tidé, Ricardo Donato, Fred Fita, Flávia Siqueira, Dani Pires **Photographer:** Rafa Motta **Client:** Mendes Júnior **Location:** Belo Horizonte, Brazil

Recepção

SALA DE

RH RECURSOS HUMANOS
COMUNICAÇÃO EMPRESARIAL
RELAÇÕES DO TRABALHO
RESPONSABILIDADE CORPORATIVA
TI TECNOLOGIA DA INFORMAÇÃO
COPA
RH RECURSOS HUMANOS
DOCUMENTOS PARA APOSENTADORIA
DESENVOLVIMENTO HUMANO
REMUNERAÇÃO, ORÇAMENTOS E CONTROLES DE RH
DIRETORIA DE RECURSOS HUMANOS
BANHEIROS
SALA DE REUNIÃO

SEBRAE-MG

SEBRAE-MG is a support agency for small businesses. The signs created for the institution are based on the pentomino puzzle. Pictograms and numbers are created from multiple combinations generated by a variety of tetris-shaped blocks. Just as scattered ideas are molded into brilliant business solutions, the playful pentomino pictograms visually exhibit the organization's mission, and transfer the brand personality into fresh and unprecedented touch points.

Design Firm: Greco Design **Designer:** Gustavo Greco, Zumberto, Tidé, João Corsino, Victor Fernandes, Alexandre Fonseca **Photographer:** Rafa Motta **Client:** SEBRAE-MG **Location:** Belo Horizonte, Brazil

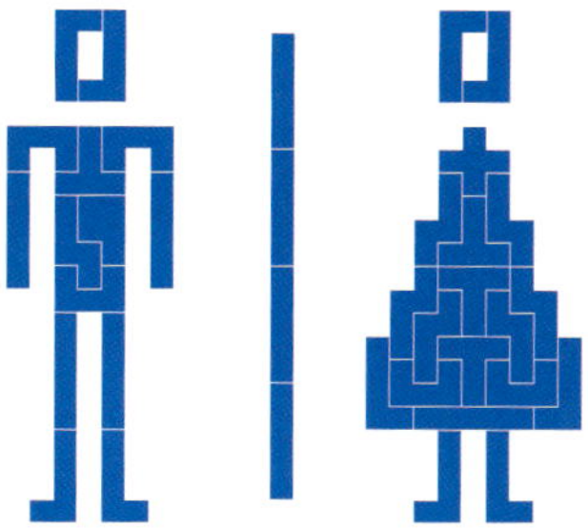

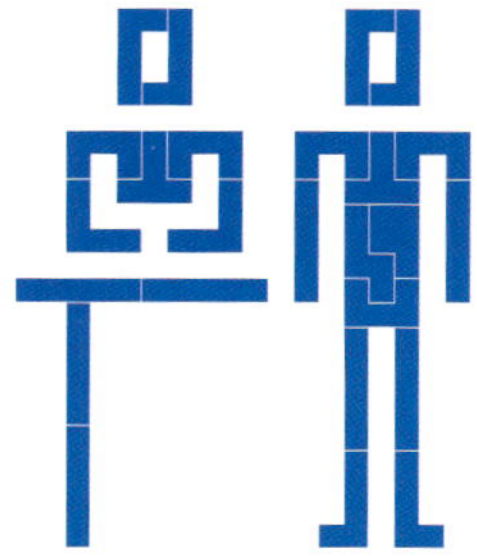

banheiro unissex recepção

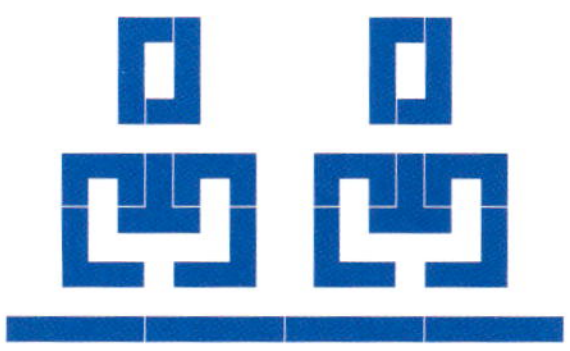

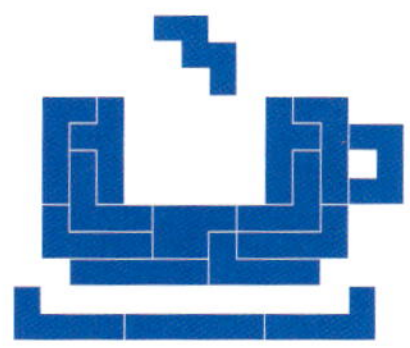

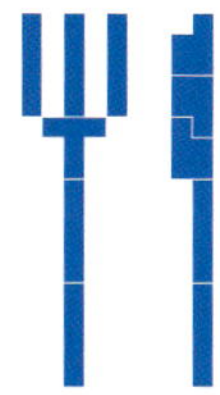

sala de reunião copa refeitório

Platinum Tower Business Complex

Located in the prime commercial area of Porto Alegre, Platinum Tower is a premium business complex which features offices, ground floor stores and three parking levels. Signs in office areas adopt metal and glassy materials to deliver a modern and efficient result. On parking levels, a mix of saturated colors working as the signage palette is applied to create a wayfinding system that is clear and eye-catching. Through a custom pictogram set, a consistent system of symbols is built and property identity is enhanced.

Design Firm: /STUDIOMDA **Designer:** Luciana Mattiello and /STUDIOMDA team **Photographer:** Marcelo Donadussi **Client:** CFL Construções
Location: Porto Alegre, RS, Brazil

platinum tower

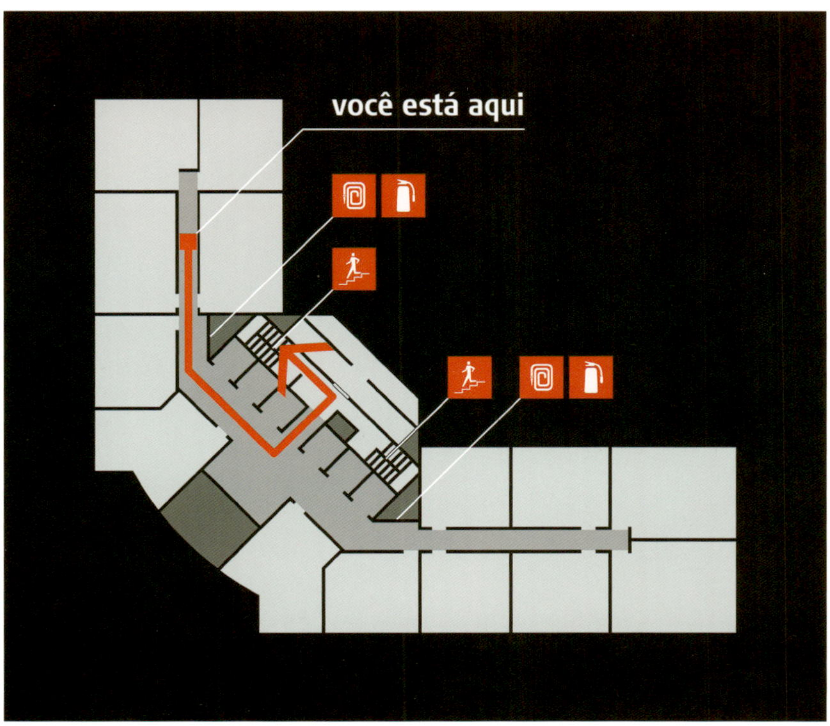
você está aqui

15
1507 a 1514
1501 a 1506

acesso elevadores
S1
S1
Você está
no nível S1

sanitário masculino

saída
saída

sanitário masculino

não fume
acesso restrito

PSJ Plaza Sor Juana

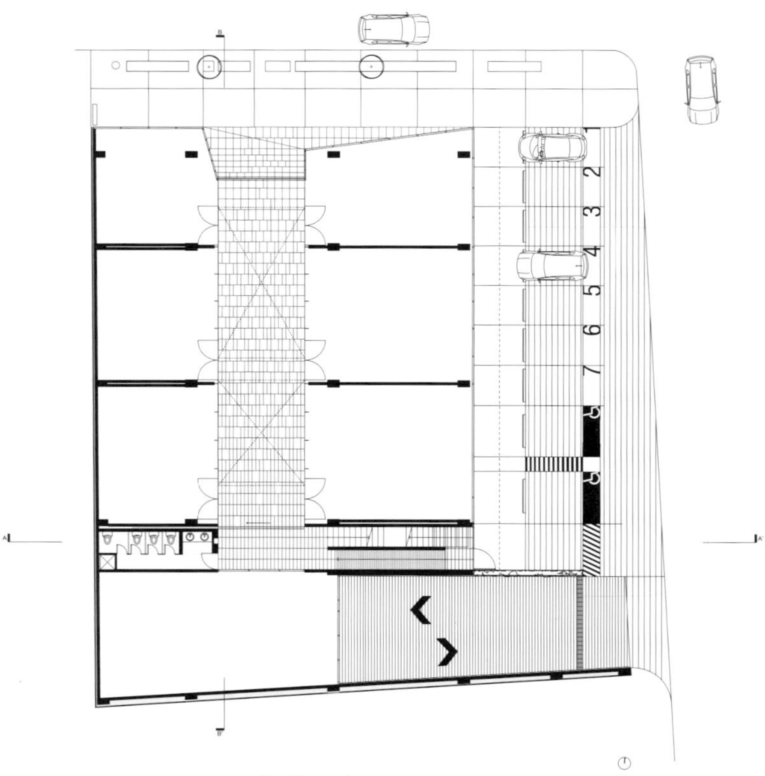

The inky walls provide a contrasting background for the white placards in this retail and office space. The exterior ground is brushed with black markers showing parking space and wheelchair accessible trails. The directions are unmistakable. It fits the visually pleasing architectural style and adds modern monochrome elements.

Design Firm: AS/D Asociación de Diseño **Designer:** Fernando Velasco, Paola Morales, Jose Munoz, Eduardo Palomino, Santiago Garcia, Piergianna Mazzocca
Photographer: Jeremy Clouser **Client:** Plaza SJ **Location:** Tlalnepantla Estado de Mexico

plaza
SOR
JUANA

a oficinas

cuarto de máquinas
35
34

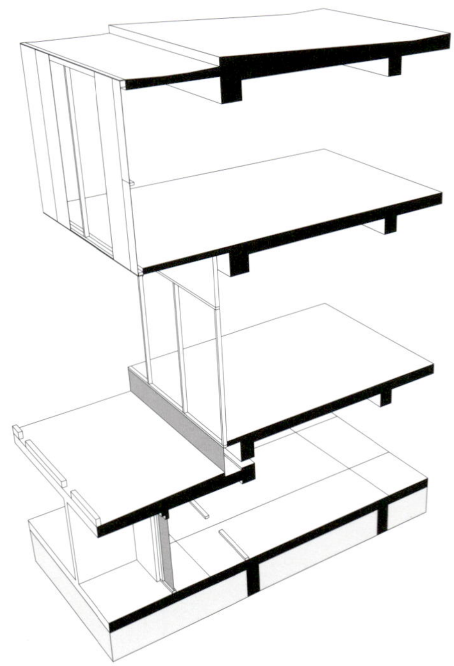

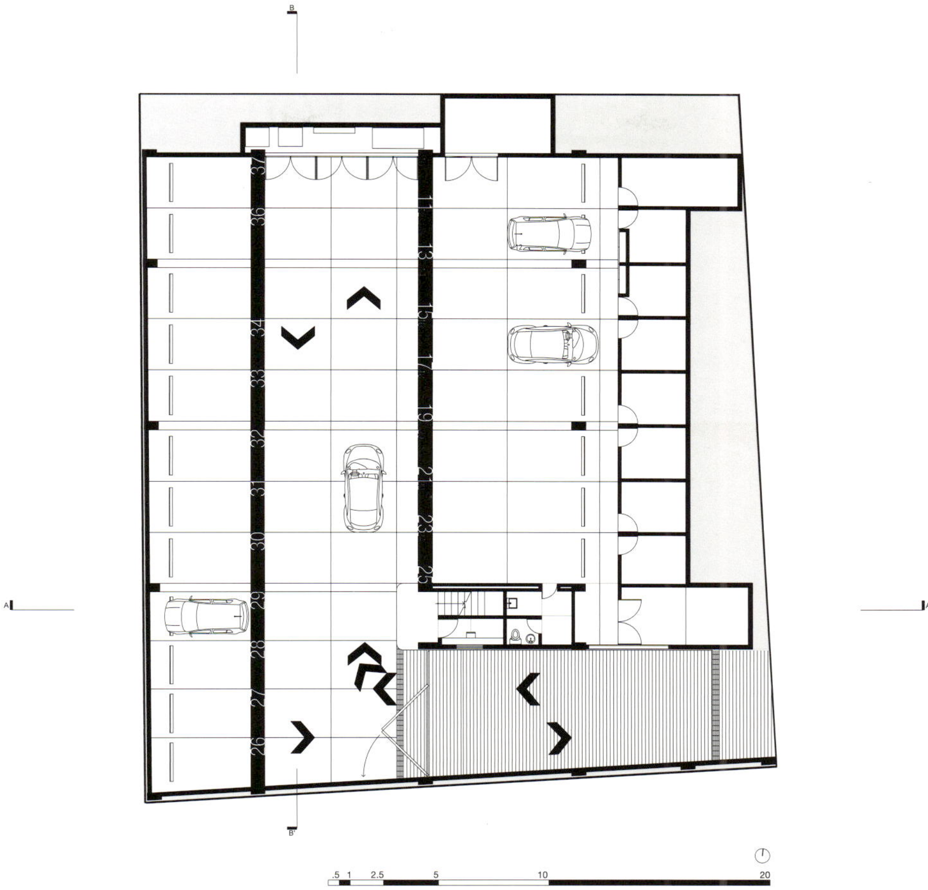
B
A
A'
B'
.5 1 2.5 5 10 20

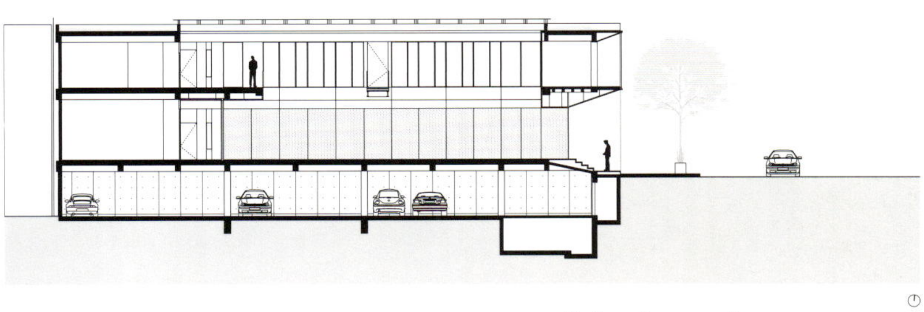
.5 1 2.5 5 10 20

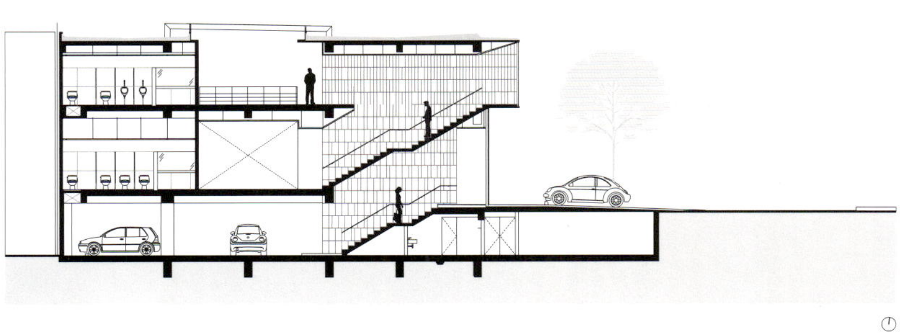
.5 1 2.5 5 10 20

DR BYEN

With five buildings clustered together, the challenge of designing a signage system for this headquarters was to visually link the different sections. Designer utilized distinct colors to categorize each zone; signage applied corresponding colors in identical, neat squares. A number of departments are united by sharing the same sign shape. As consistency and clarity are implemented in signage, a pleasing corporation identity is reinforced.

Design Firm: Studio Alavi **Designer:** Masoud Alavi **Photographer:** Masoud Alavi **Client:** Danish Broadcasting Corporation **Location:** Copenhagen, Denmark

DR BYEN
← 7 9

3
UD 5 8 →
← 1 2 4

2

1 2 5 8
3 7 9
6

LOKALE
4202-04
TEKNIKOMRÅDE STUDIE 14

STUDIE
14

LEISURE SPACE

Wayfinding in Leisure Spaces: A Personalized and Cultured Flavor

Leisure space, which includes clubs, museums, theaters and exhibition centers, aim at creating a relaxed and cultured place which will resonate with visitors who go for recreation and arts.

Unlike business-related or administrative locations, the main target users of wayfinding systems in cultural spheres enjoy a more artistic taste. The signage design for this field requires sensibility and aesthetics to please such refined palate. This high demand of artistic value distinguishes the signage design philosophy in cultivated domains from their less sophisticated counterparts and gives us a fresh taste of esthetic wayfinding projects.

Trade Fair Innsbruck

Innsbruck, the formerly characterless exhibition center, now has a new identity: a harmonious vibe has overridden what used to be a cacophony. The previous chaotic muddle of juxtaposed wayfinding languages and routes through the complex has been resolved in a new signage project that stems from the ideas of flag design.

Inspirations from national flags form the basis of the graphic design. Those Flags' heraldic elements and color schemes have been replaced by a single color shade along with text. The individual text-patterns are assigned to particular halls where they fulfill their designated wayfinding functions. When the text-patterns are lined up together in the overviews, the individual patterns become parts of a different, larger system. Guiding strips in bright colors make a bold statement, echoing with the non-uniformity of the dazzling signage setting. The structural simplicity of the basic two-color composition in graphic design adapts to the variety of surfaces, materials and colors in the halls.

The signage constitutes a systematic chaos, an orderly disorder, which reflects the venue's intrinsic disorderly qualities. In the neatly dimensioned and relatively monochrome building, the design adds contrast and variation, providing rhythmic elements that naturally expand to cover whole walls of the center.

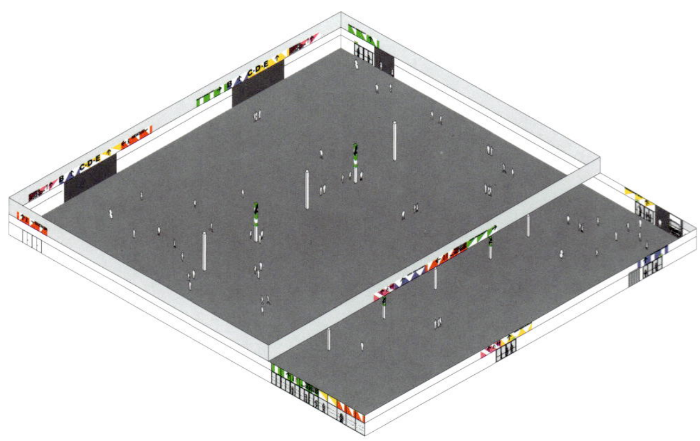

Design Firm: büro uebele visuelle kommunikation **Designer:** Carolin Himmel, Andreas Uebele **Architect:** ARGE Cukrowicz Nachbaur Bechter Zaffignani Marte
Photographer: Hanspeter Schiess **Client:** Congress und Messe Innsbruck GmbH **Location:** Innsbruck, Austria

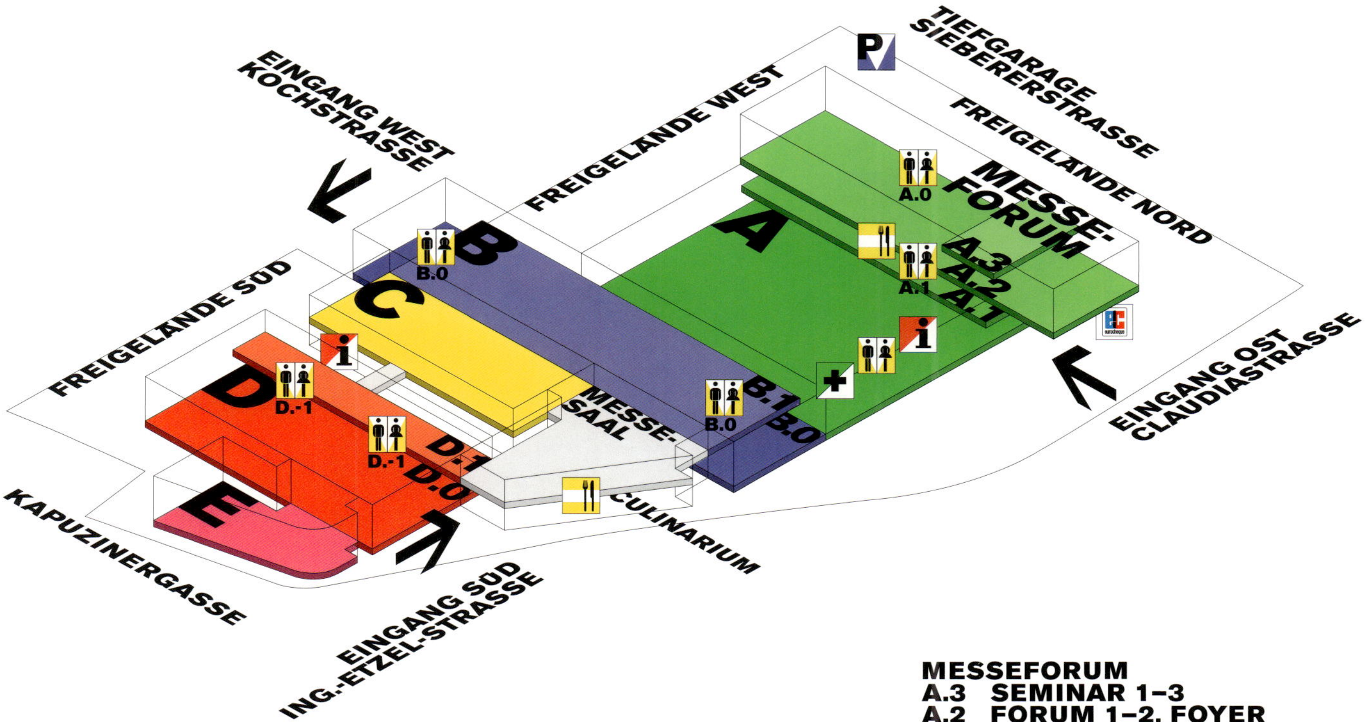

MESSEFORUM
A.3 SEMINAR 1–3
A.2 FORUM 1–2, FOYER
A.1 RESTAURANT

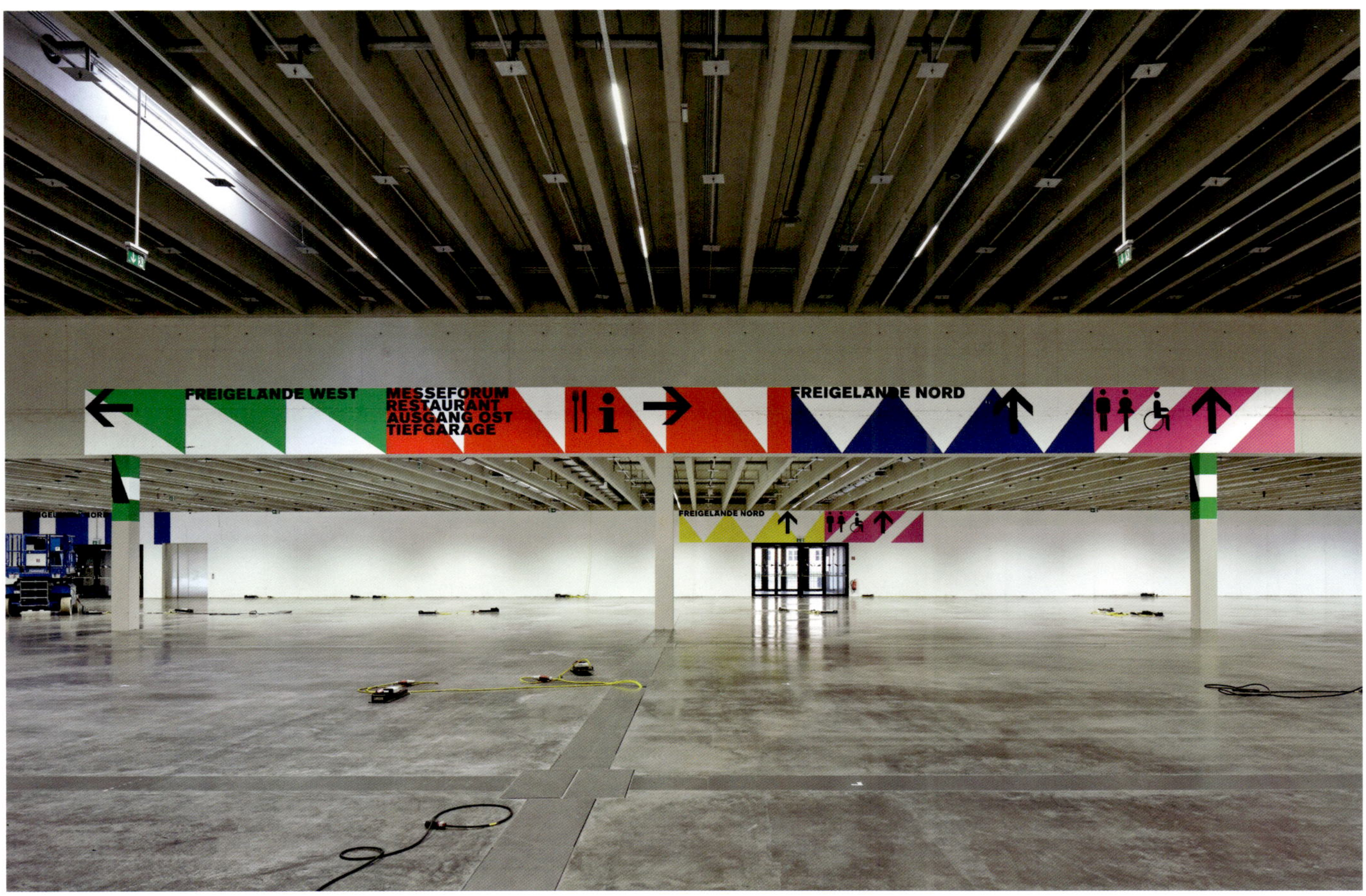

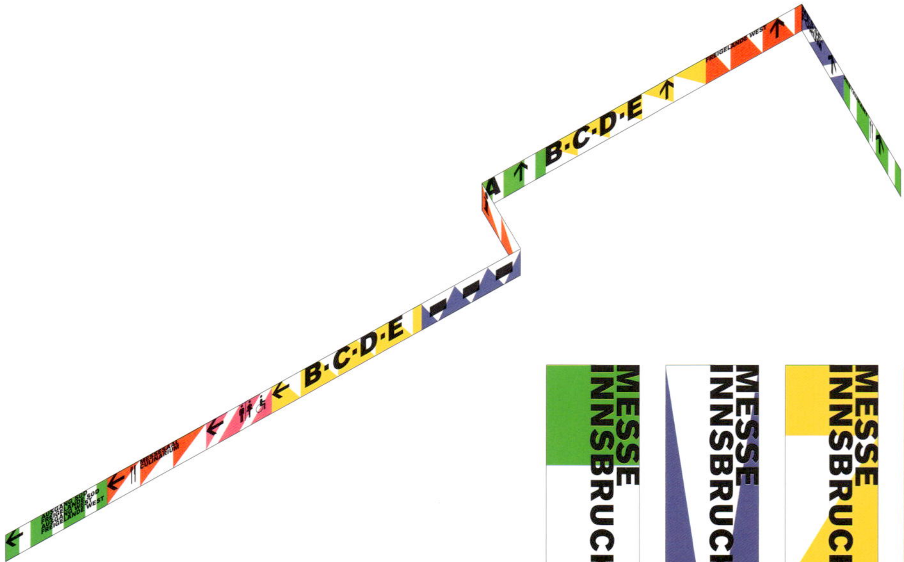
A
B·C·D·E
B·C·D·E

MESSE INNSBRUCK
MESSE INNSBRUCK
MESSE INNSBRUCK
MESSE INNSBRUCK
MESSE INNSBRUCK

A·B
MESSESAAL
MESSEFORUM
FREIGELÄNDE NORD
AUSGANG OST
TIEFGARAGE
SIEBERERSTRASSE
AUSGANG SÜD
D

AUSGANG
WEST
FREIGELÄNDE
SÜD
FREIGELÄNDE
WEST
A
B.0

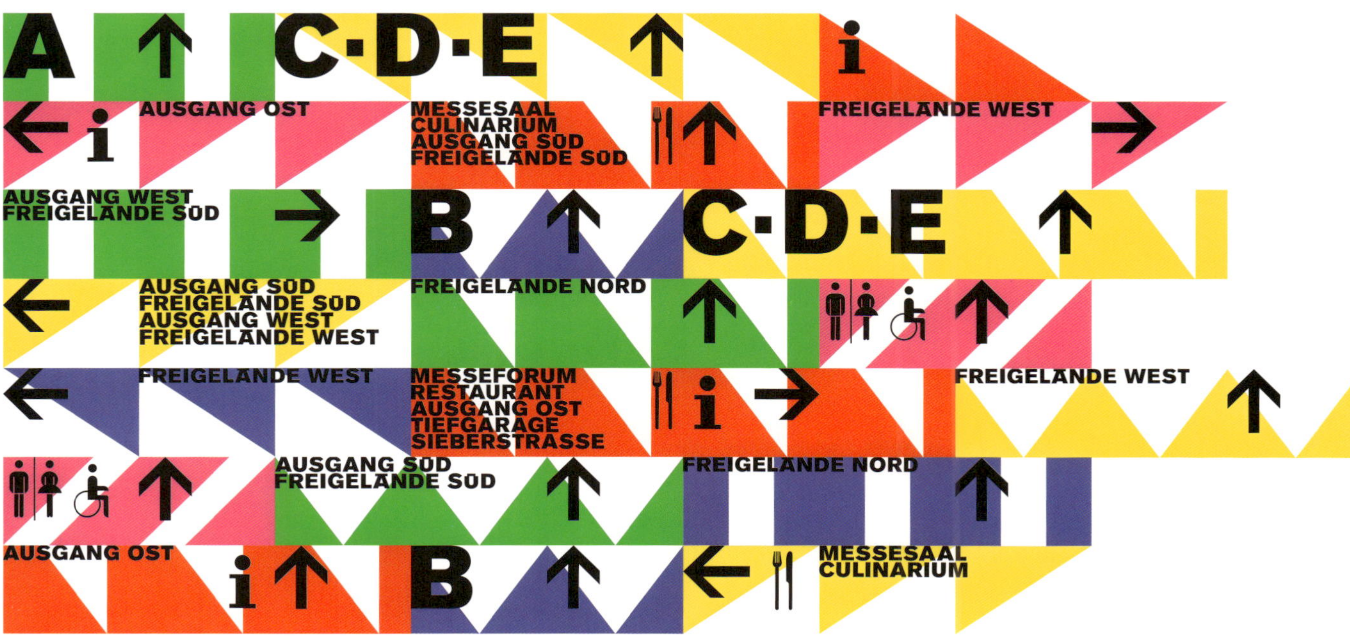
A
C·D·E
AUSGANG OST
MESSESAAL
CULINARIUM
AUSGANG SÜD
FREIGELÄNDE SÜD
FREIGELÄNDE WEST
AUSGANG WEST
FREIGELÄNDE SÜD
B
C·D·E
AUSGANG SÜD
FREIGELÄNDE SÜD
AUSGANG WEST
FREIGELÄNDE WEST
FREIGELÄNDE NORD
FREIGELÄNDE WEST
MESSEFORUM
RESTAURANT
AUSGANG OST
TIEFGARAGE
SIEBERSTRASSE
FREIGELÄNDE WEST
AUSGANG SÜD
FREIGELÄNDE SÜD
FREIGELÄNDE NORD
AUSGANG OST
B
MESSESAAL
CULINARIUM

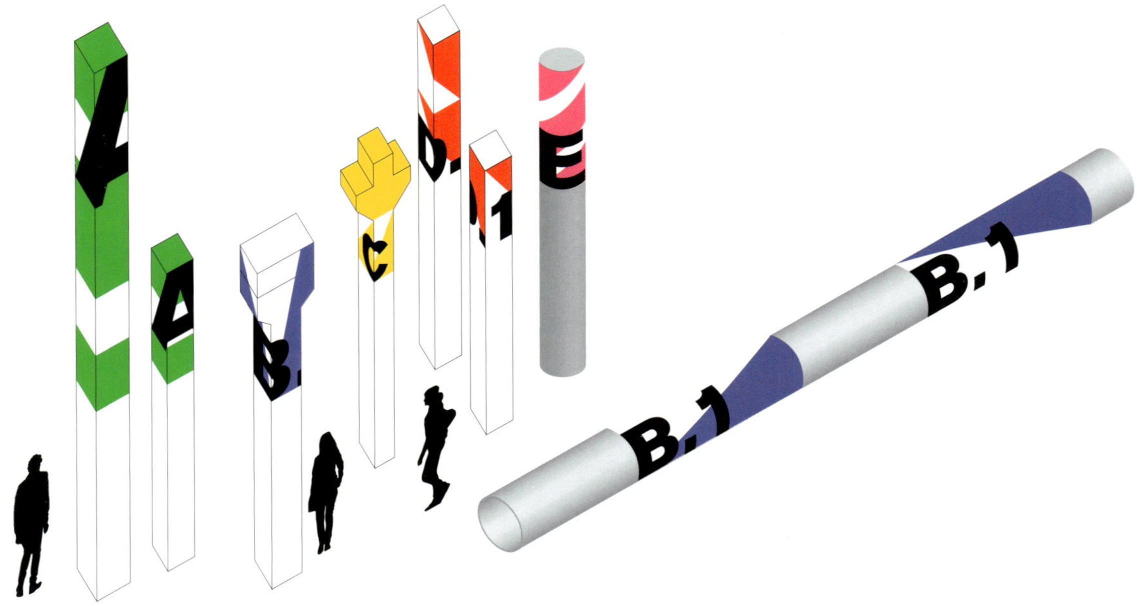
B.1
B.1

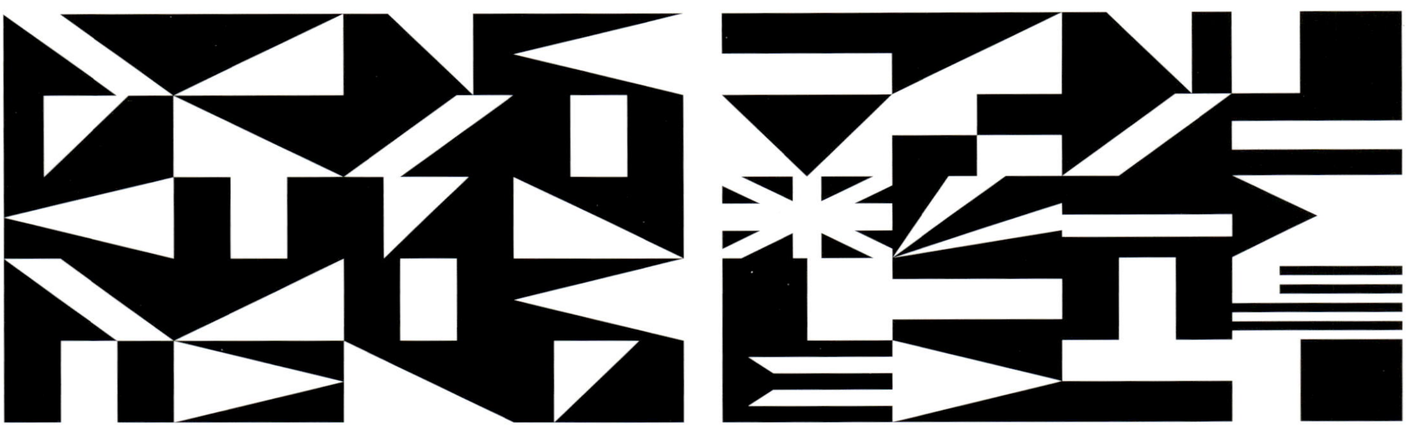

A
B·C·D·E
A.1·A.2·A.3

SÜD
T
WEST
MESSESAAL
CULINARIUM

Lisbon Story Centre

The exhibition building which presents the history of the Lisbon city employs a wayfinding system that is naturally integrated with the sensory and interactive experience created by its interior design. Clean-cut signage is put on the walls in contrasting and soothing colors, elegantly navigating explorers. On the outside, the wayfinding is combined with big graphics decorating the façade, inviting people to enjoy this poetic story center.

Design Firm: P-06 Atelier **Designer:** Pedro Anjos, Vanda Mota **Photographer:** Ricardo Gonçalves **Client:** HCI - Construções, S. A **Location:** Lisbon, Portugal

PISO FLOOR 1
EXPOSIÇÕES TEMPORÁRIAS
TEMPORARY EXHIBITIONS
SALAS DE ACTIVIDADES
ACTIVITY ROOMS
PISO FLOOR 0
EXPOSIÇÃO EXHIBITION

EXPOSIÇÃO
SAÍDA

National Museum of Natural History and Science

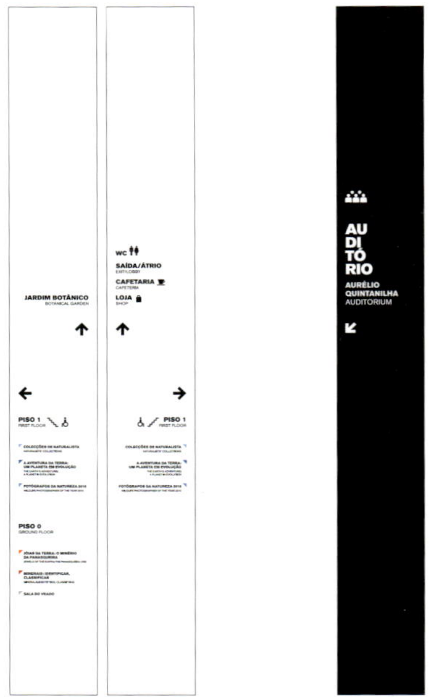

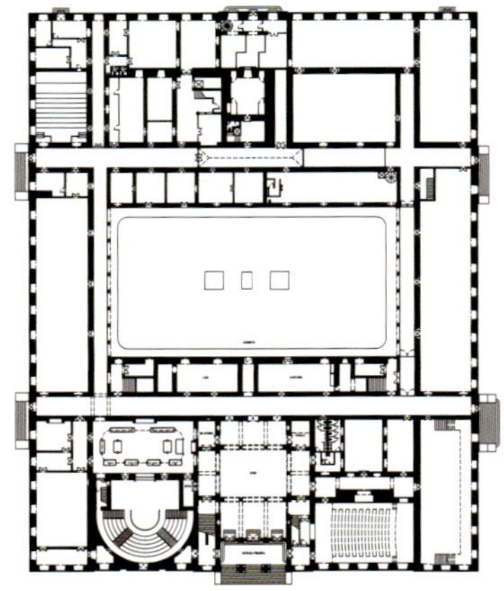

Piso 0

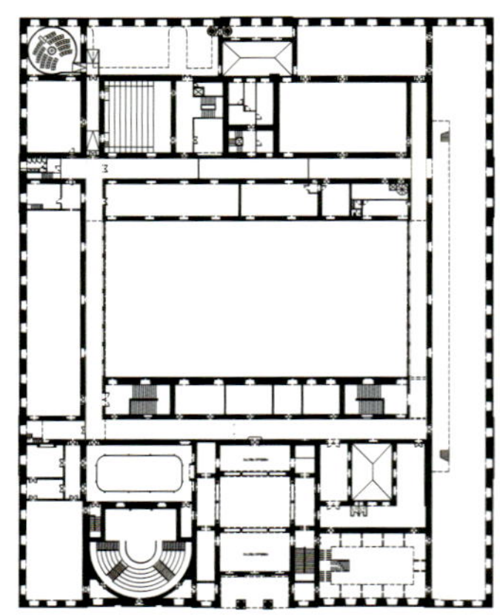

Piso 1

Design Firm: P-06 Atelier **Designer:** Nuno Gusmão, Pedro Anjos, Joana Proserpio, Mário Videira, Vanda Mota, Giuseppe Greco

Photographer: João Morgado, Ricardo Gonçalves **Client:** University of Lisbon **Location:** Lisbon, Portugal

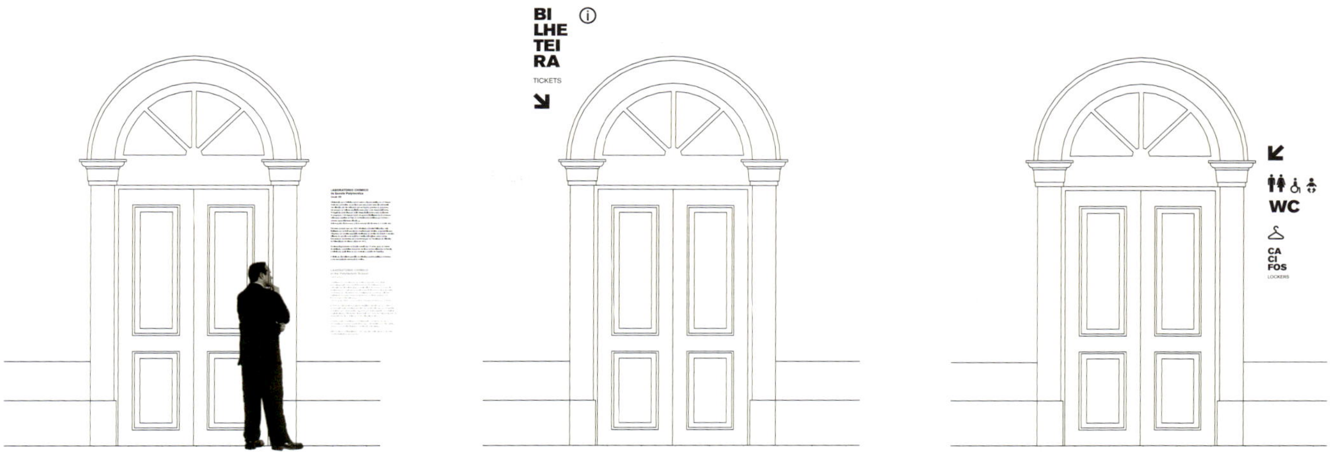

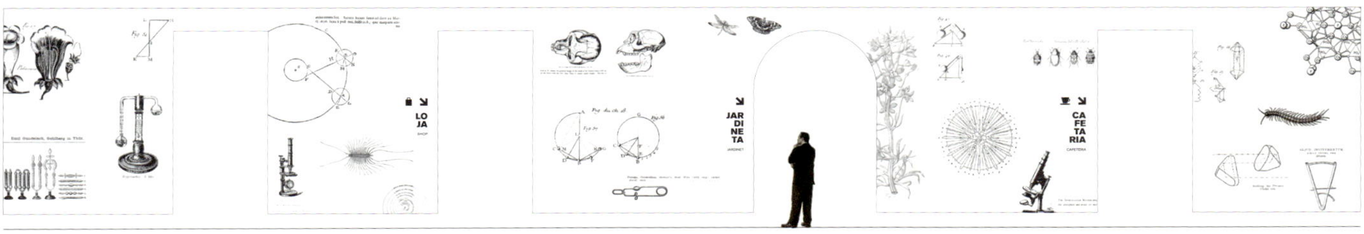

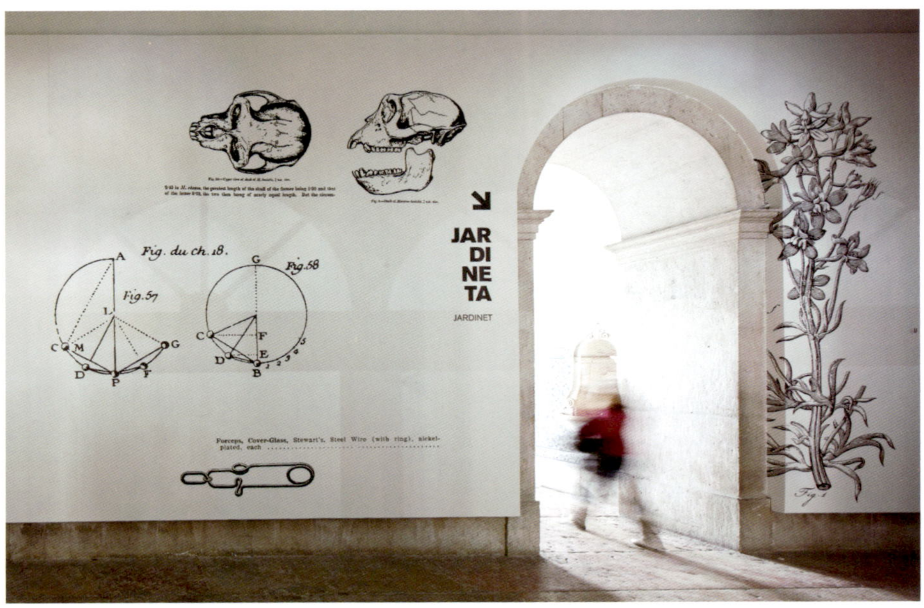

A graceful signage system was developed to promote exhibits in this National Museum. The exterior signage consists of two large, three-dimensional images covering the façade to show the contents of the exhibitions from a distance. Along the indoor corridors, signage information is printed on independent paper screens or walls in clear white and black. The combination of the wayfinding system and the distinctive wall graphics about nature makes the museum a sparkling and gentle space filled with charm.

National Library of Bucharest

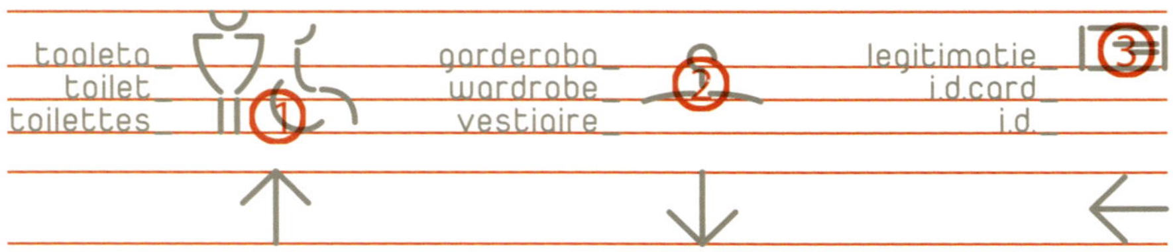

Based on straight lines and geometries, an innovative and minimalist icon design was crafted to adorn the signage system for the largest national library in Romania. Emerging from a basic metric grid combined with circles and diagonals, the pictograms present linear shapes and round visual effects; the icons and languages are well arranged in a dynamic and flexible way to form wayfinding signs. The designer adopts the duepuntozero font in both texts and pictograms, uniting the signage elements and making icons more like dingbats. In the bright areas, information in neutral black on the white wall provides high contrast while in the darker areas the designer uses neon tubes in white light to enlighten the signage.

This trim and artistic signage design not only facilitates orientation in a clear style, but also adds intellectual touches to this cultured library.

Designer: Andreea Mihaiu **Photographer:** Adrian Mihaiu **Client:** The National Library **Location:** Bucharest, Romania

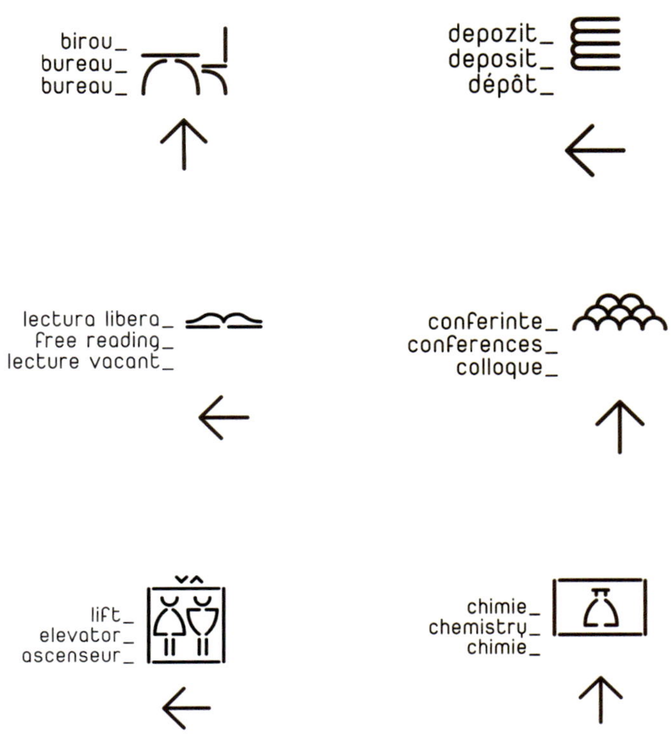

Biblioteca
Națională
București

Copernicus Science Center

Irregular contours in the open architectural plans of the Copernicus Science Center inspired the shapes of its signage icons. The designer created a set of distinct pictograms in a lively, variant style. The wayfinding repeats the irregular shapes of the pictograms to maintain further consistency. Maps placed on the blocks help visitors quickly find their locational objectives. Minimal use of colors, simplicity and consistency of signage ensure visibility on the multi-colored background of numerous exhibitions. The resulting signage presented in two languages effectively assists people in wayfinding without overwhelming them or distracting them from the exhibitions. It also further highlights the building's open structure and surroundings in a clear, yet subtle manner.

Design Firm: Mamastudio **Designer:** Magda Ponagajbo, Piotr Stolarski **Photographer:** Nicolas Grospierre **Client:** Copernicus Science Center **Location:** Warsaw, Poland

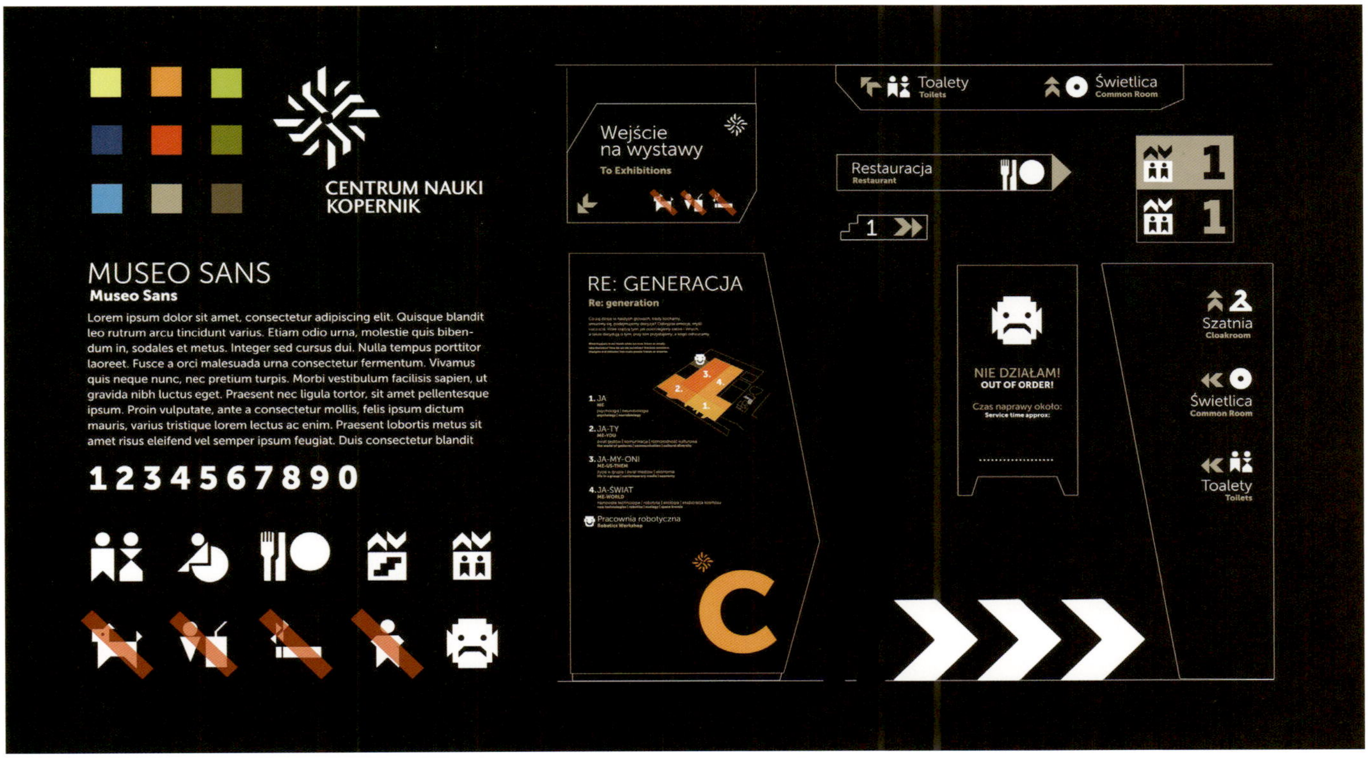
CENTRUM NAUKI
KOPERNIK
MUSEO SANS
Museo Sans
Lorem ipsum dolor sit amet, consectetur adipiscing elit. Quisque blandit leo rutrum arcu tincidunt varius. Etiam odio urna, molestie quis bibendum in, sodales et metus. Integer sed cursus dui. Nulla tempus porttitor laoreet. Fusce a orci malesuada urna consectetur fermentum. Vivamus quis neque nunc, nec pretium turpis. Morbi vestibulum facilisis sapien, ut gravida nibh luctus eget. Praesent nec ligula tortor, sit amet pellentesque ipsum. Proin vulputate, ante a consectetur mollis, felis ipsum dictum mauris, varius tristique lorem lectus ac enim. Praesent lobortis metus sit amet risus eleifend vel semper ipsum feugiat. Duis consectetur blandit
1234567890
Wejście na wystawy
To Exhibitions
Toalety
Toilets
Świetlica
Common Room
Restauracja
Restaurant
1
RE: GENERACJA
Re: generation
NIE DZIAŁAM!
OUT OF ORDER!
Czas naprawy około:
Service time approx:
Szatnia
Cloakroom
Świetlica
Common Room
Toalety
Toilets
C

PLANETARIUM
O

Wejście
na wystawy
To Exhibitions
Obiekt
monitorowany
Monitoring

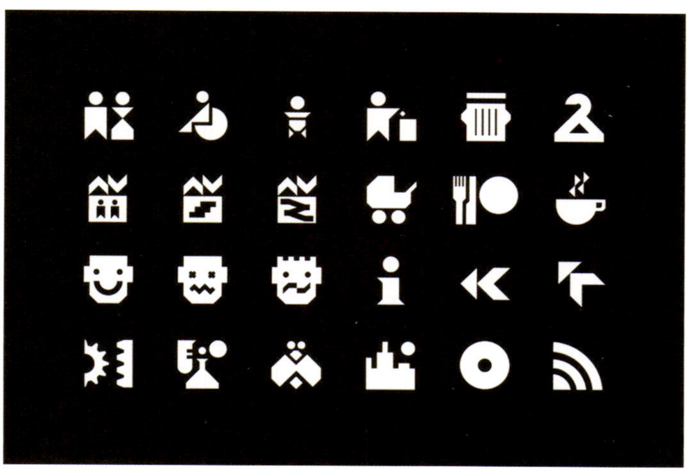

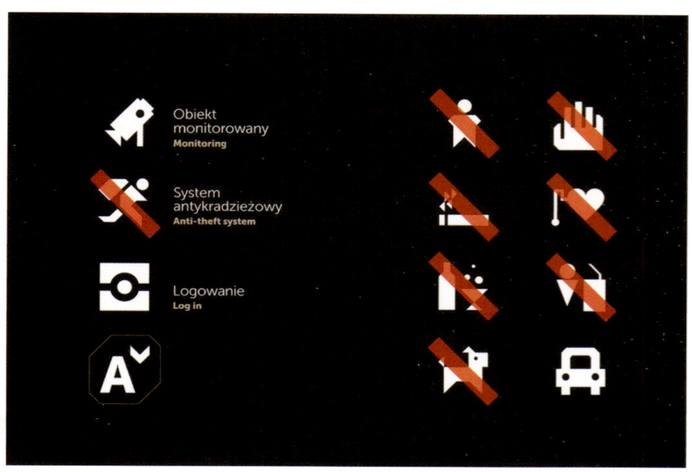
Obiekt
monitorowany
Monitoring
System
antykradzieżowy
Anti-theft system
Logowanie
Log in

Toalety
Toilets

Salonik
Common Room
Szatnia
Cloakroom
Salonik
Common Room
Toalety
Toilets

Feevale Theater

The wayfinding solution for the theater of Feevale University is based on the school's visual identity. The signage of four floors and seven parking levels is united through a gradation from yellow to green, which are colors constituting the school's brand. With the intention of personalizing a universal and easily understood set of icons, the designer created a series of pictograms stylizing the AIGA/DOT system. The theater's identity is boosted as its theme colors are planted into the signage system.

Design Firm: /STUDIOMDA **Designer:** Luciana Mattiello and /STUDIOMDA team **Photographer:** Marcelo Donadussi **Client:** Feevale University
Location: Novo Hamburgo, Brazil

6b
VAGAS
VELOCIDADE
MÁXIMA
10km/h
SAÍDA

FILAS A a L
rows A to L
PLATEIA LADO ÍMPAR
stalls odd number seats
PLATEIA LADO PAR
stalls even number seats
FILAS A a L
rows A to L
ELEVADORES
elevators
SANITÁRIOS
restrooms

SANITÁRIOS
restrooms
SANITÁRIO FAMILIAR
family restroom
FRALDÁRIO
baby changing station

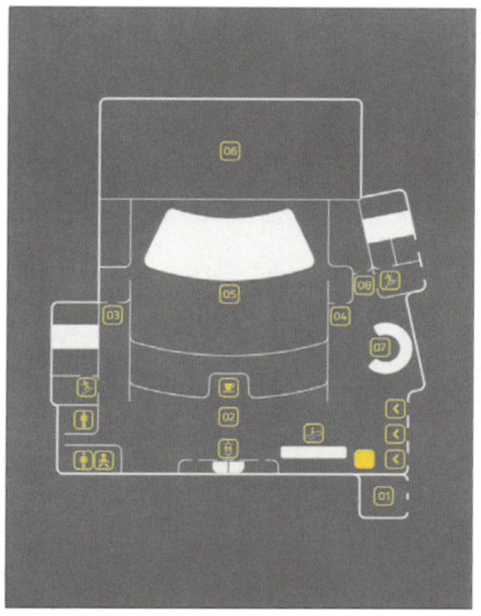

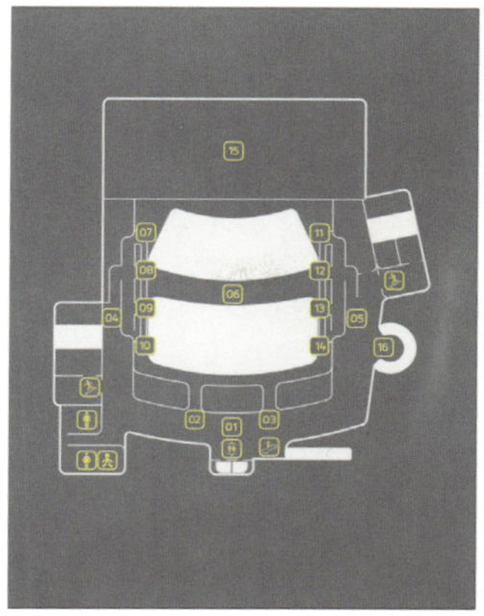

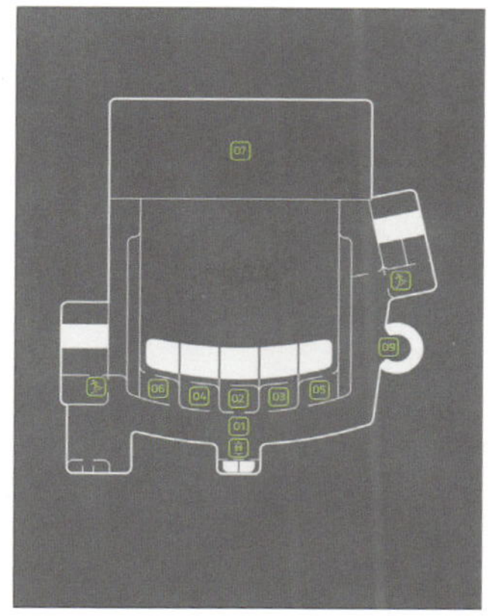

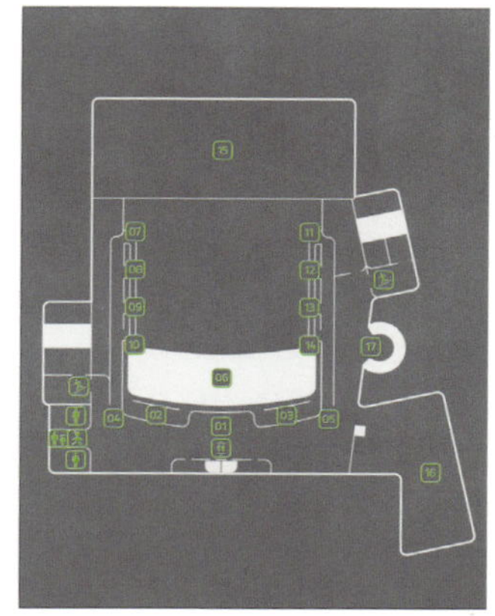

3a

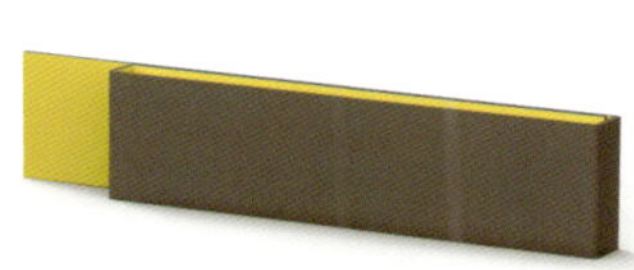

The Museum of Byzantine Culture

The museum presents various aspects of life during Byzantine periods. To accomplish this, its signage system implements a set of mosaic icons recreated in three dimensions by real mosaic stones in a similar style to the fabulous Byzantine mosaics. The subtly-colored monolithic information boards are shaped with rectangles indicating directions by angles. The designers adopted the modification of the H&FJ Whitney typeface with additional glyphs and ligatures to create a unique branded typographic system. An artistic work in itself, this antique signage design flavours the museum and spontaneously activates Byzantine culture.

Design Firm: Beetroot Design Group **Client:** The Museum of Byzantine Culture **Location:** Thessaloniki, Greece

ΜΟΥΣΕΙΟ
ΒΥΖΑΝΤΙΝΟΥ
ΠΟΛΙΤΙΣΜΟΥ
MUSEUM
OF BYZANTINE
CULTURE

ΚΑΦΕ
ΕΣΤΙΑΤΟΡΙΟ
Café - Restaurant
WC

PROJECT

Museum of Byzantine Culture wayfinding system

10018

Graphic Design / Wayfinding

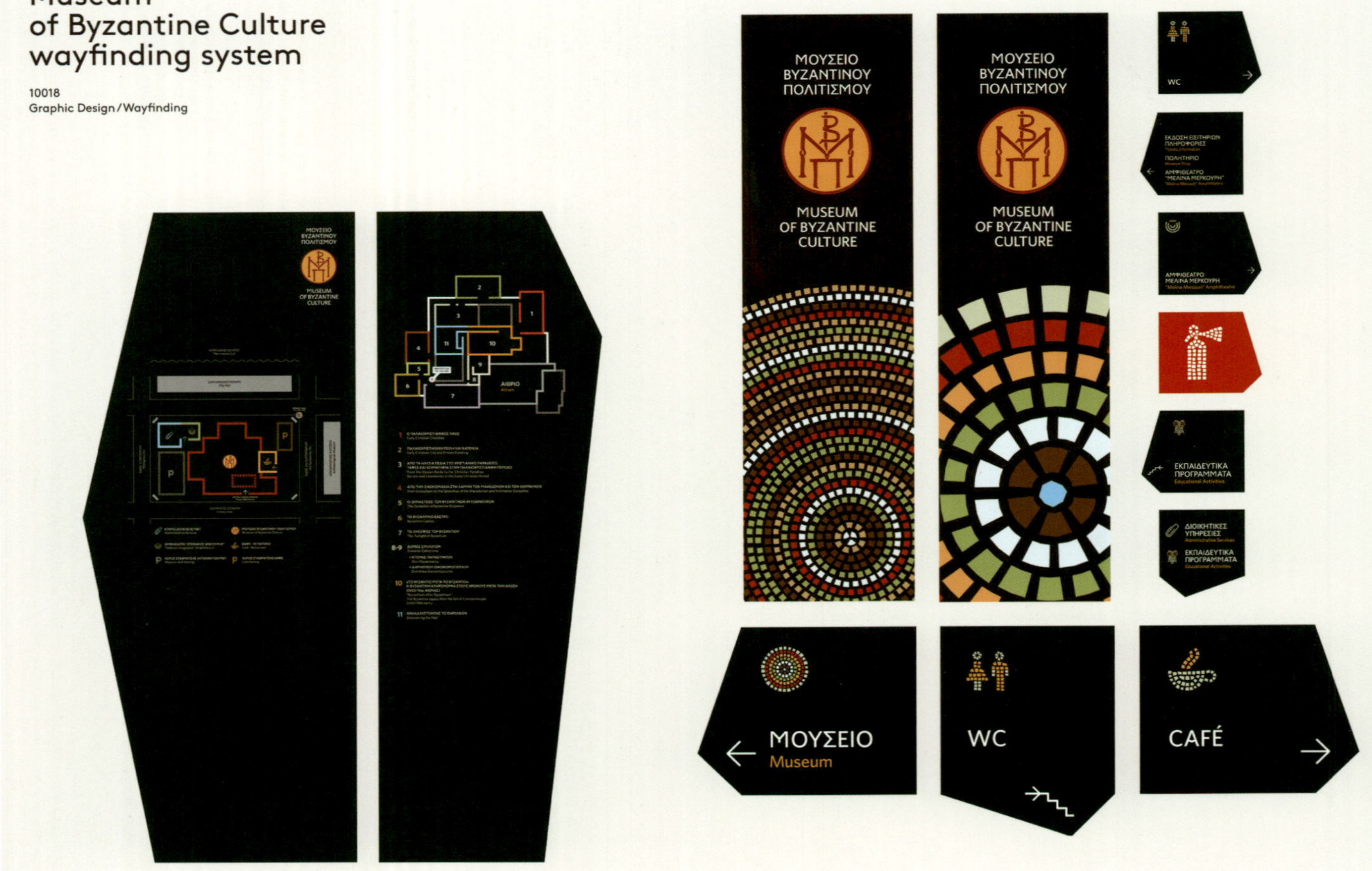

ΕΚΔΟΣΗ ΕΙΣΙΤΗΡΙΩΝ
ΠΛΗΡΟΦΟΡΙΕΣ
Tickets, Information
ΠΩΛΗΤΗΡΙΟ
Museum Shop
ΑΜΦΙΘΕΑΤΡΟ
"ΜΕΛΙΝΑ ΜΕΡΚΟΥΡΗ"
"Melina Mercouri" Amphitheatre
CCTV
NO SMOKING
ΚΑΦΕ - ΕΣΤΙΑΤΟΡΙΟ
Café - Restaurant

ΠΩΛΗΤΗΡΙΟ
Museum Shop

Nine Degrees Spa

Design Firm: Esadore International **Designer:** Mohammad Hamed Zeinali **Client:** Nine Degrees Spa **Location:** Dubai, United Arab Emirates

Relying on simplicity and universally comprehension, an easy family of pictograms was created for this unique spa brand. The designer applied light blue and white in the signage system to reflect a carefree spa environment where people can relax. The simple lines in the iconology design make it effortless for customers to navigate, naturally harmonizing with the fresh colors. The wayfinding system on the wall clearly and instantly communicates while catering to the interior design and reinforcing the brand concept of providing an enjoyable spa.

Times Museum

The designer tailored a bilingual stencil lettering system for Times Museum. Both stainless-steel sign boards and graphics painted on concrete walls and floors adopt this lettering design. The floor information covers the lift door in a hand-drawn style and decorates this artistic interior space. The signage system uses stainless materials and laser-cut lettering in silver and grey to release a modern industrial sense.

Design Firm: 250 Gramm **Designer:** Nivard Thoes **Photographer:** 250 Gramm **Client:** Guangdong Museum of Art **Location:** Guangzhou, China

顶楼
办公室
首层
地下层

电梯
ELEVATORS
露台
TERRACE
WEST
EAST

展厅

Phoenix Square

The wayfinding system of this art center includes interior wall graphics and a wall map which uses raised printing. The project directs the crowds while encouraging them to explore the Cube Gallery: a digital art gallery commonly neglected by visitors. By referencing electronic circuits, designers created varicolored lines that traverse the space—passing through doorways and around corners—inspiring visitors to explore all sections of the building. In addition to the main signage graphics, an illustrated map was used to exhibit the local sites of Phoenix. Notable buildings are marked by different colors in perspex blocks. This map gives visitors a vivid and colorful overview of the neighborhood.

Through the dynamic pattern of lines conducting guests through the interior labyrinth, the signage system naturally guides guests through the space and infuses positive thinking into this art center.

Design Firm: Un.titled **Designer:** Abi Harrison, Jake Hutchinson **Photographer:** Eden Morse **Client:** Phoenix **Location:** Leicester, UK

Box office
Phoenix
Welcome to Leicester's
independent cinema,
art centre and café bar

Your Phoenix

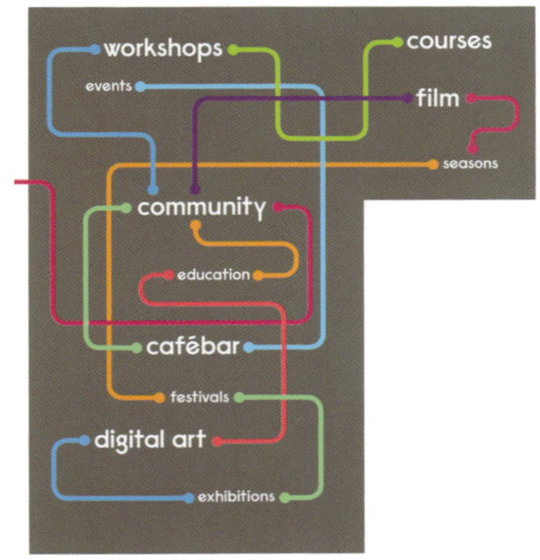
workshops
courses
events
film
seasons
community
education
cafébar
festivals
digital art
exhibitions

events
courses
film
seasons
community
Your Phoenix
education
cafébar
festivals
digital art
exhibitions
BUSTER KEATON'S
THE GENERAL

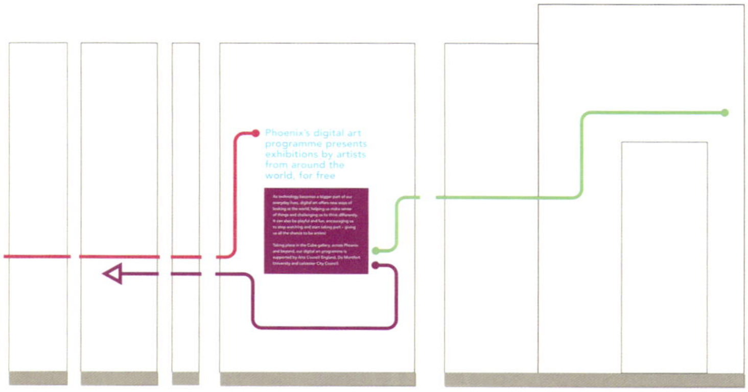
Phoenix's digital art programme presents exhibitions by artists from around the world, for free

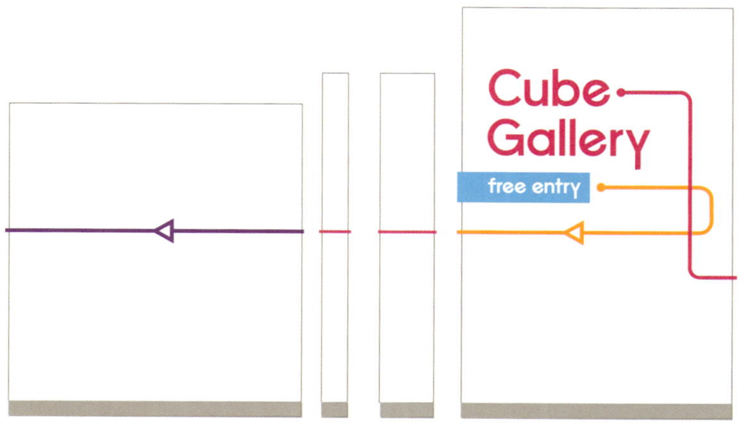
Cube Gallery
free entry

Cube Gallery
Cube Gallery
free entry

Cube Gallery
Phoenix's digital art programme presents exhibitions by artists from around the world, for free
As technology becomes a bigger part of our everyday lives, digital art offers new ways of looking at the world, helping us make sense of things and challenging us to think differently. It can also be playful and fun, encouraging us to stop watching and start taking part – giving us all the chance to be artists!
Taking place in the Cube gallery, across Phoenix and beyond, our digital art programme is supported by Arts Council England, De Montfort University and Leicester City Council.
DE MONTFORT UNIVERSITY
ARTS COUNCIL ENGLAND

Humberstone Gate
J Herbert Music
Vestry Street
Rutland Street
Curve
Yeoman Street
Southampton Street
Halford Street
Wigston Street
Queen Street
Athena
9
10
11
8
2
3
5
7
6

St Georges App—
Cultural Quarter Trail

Screen 1

Screen 2

Voskresenskoe Center

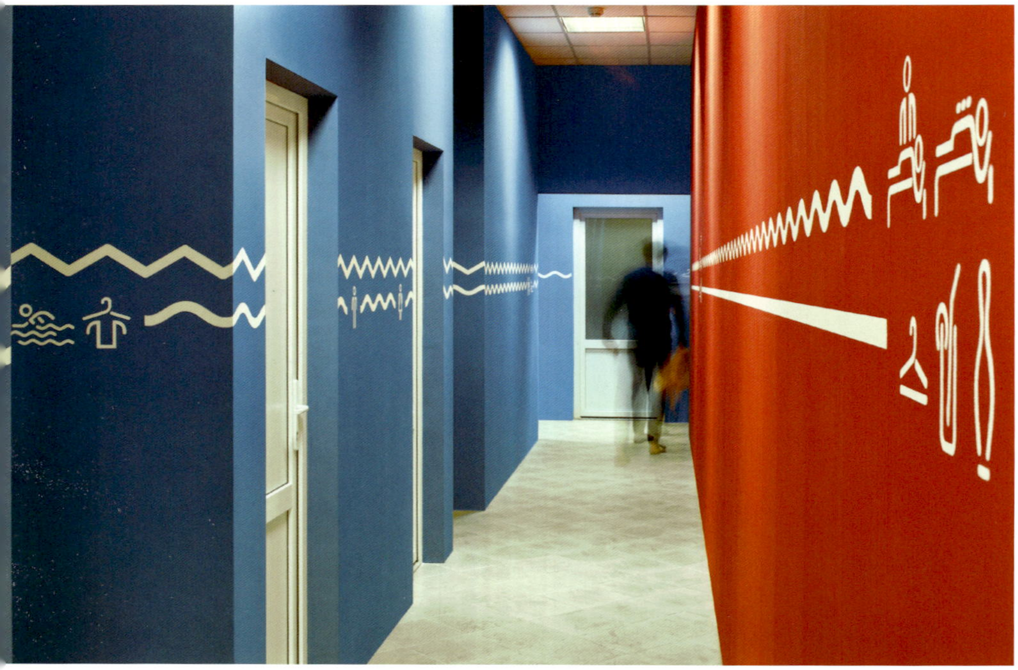

The designer created a comfortable navigation system leading to its fitness center. The wayfinding system utilizes bright colors to achieve better orientation and build a lighthearted background. Pictograms and wayfinding elements are placed on the walls with wavy graphics, which are an additional element of the original wayfinding system. They lead visitors all the way to their destination and visualize the rhythm of sports.

Design Firm: Tomat design **Designer:** Farhad Kucharov **Location:** Moscow, Russia

Toiro Wayfinding

Toiro is a multi-use rental development with a bright visual impression. The concise wayfinding system was designed to specifically suit the Toiro atmosphere. In accordance with this company's logo, the signs add clarity to the environment, emphasizing the concepts of minimalism and inclusiveness.

Design Firm: Kamitopen Architecture Design Office co., ltd. **Designer:** Masahiro Yoshida, Jin Hatanaka, Riyo-Tsuhata **Photographer:** Keisuke Miyamoto
Client: Saitama arena **Location:** Saitama, Japan

EXHIBITION
5
3
SPACE
TOIRO

2
STUDIO
1
STUDIO

2
STUDIO
STUDIO 2
1
STUDIO
STUDIO 1

BUSINESS
SYMPOSIUM
SPACE 5
FORUM
4
SPACE

FAX
ビジネスセンター
BUSINESS CENTER

ROOM 6
6
ROOM

The Library in Copenhagen

The wayfinding system for the new public library uses bold typography painted directly on the surface to avoid cluttering the stretched metal walls. This concept is supplemented by a series of black aluminum signs on each floor and texts on all doors. The shelf signage is custom-made to fit the layout of each library department, and match the visual style of the wayfinding signs.

Design Firm: Rama Studio **Photographer:** Rama Studio **Client:** City of Copenhagen **Location:** Copenhagen, Denmark

SALEN
TERRASSEN
VOKSEN
UNG/MEDIER
PERSONALE

3. SAL
SALEN
TERRASSEN
Toiletter
SALEN/A
SA
VÆRKSTE

76
BIB
LIO
TEK
ET
BIBLIOTEK
KULTURHUS
BORGERSERVICE KVIK
CAFE GLAD
BISPEBJERG LOKALUDVALG
VÆRKSTEDER
LOKAL-TV / LOKALRADIO
MEDBORGERCENTER

PEGEBØGER
EVENTYR
FANTASY/SCI-FI
ROMANER
FILOSOFI
SAMFUNDET
10
30
A
B
DVD BØRN
DVD VOKSNE
SPIL WII
H—N
A—G
AVANTGARDE
JAZZ ANTOLOGIER
90 HISTORIE
TRANSPORT
DYR
A
B
XYZ

EVENTYR

B
TRANSPORT

Magion Library

The library in Grindsted has a radiant visual identity through its logo, signage and foyer decoration. Seven lighted signs indicate the primary areas in the library's large main hall. The signs are visible from the whole floor due to their high placement. Their visibility offers easy navigation and enables the staff to clearly point out specific areas to visitors. The space calls for large and clear signs for the primary shelves. These signs are readable from a distance.

The signage system doubles as a functional guide and decorative enhancement, lightening the library and providing a cheerful reading environment.

Design Firm: Rama Studio **Photographer:** Rama Studio **Client:** City of Grindsted **Location:** Grindsted, Denmark

TWEENS

TÅRNET
TÅRNET

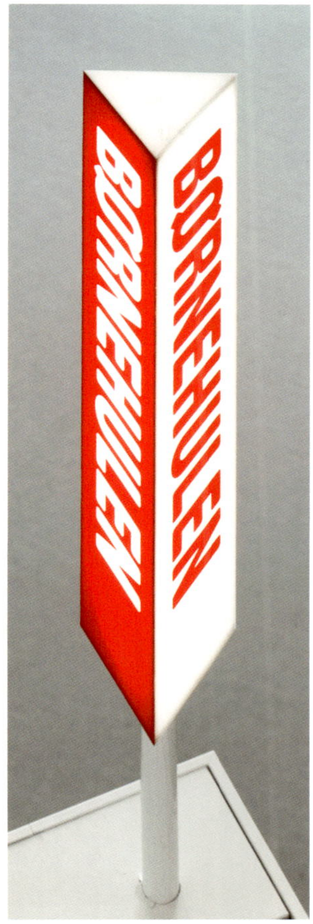
BØRNEHULEN
BØRNEHULEN

KVIK

Det er en almindelig udbredt opfattelse, at en velhavende ungkarl absolut må mangle en kone.
Jane Austen: Stolthed og fordom.
NØJ DET ER FOR BØRN
ANNA OG LOTTE
DANMARKS RADIO
YOU TALKIN' TO ME?
ROBERT DE NIRO, TAXI DRIVER
DO I FEEL LUCKY? WELL DO YA, PUNK?
CLINT EASTWOOD, DIRTY HARRY.
CLICK. BOOM. AMAZING!
STEVE JOBS.
MAGION BIBLIO TEKET

Obro Jagtvej Library

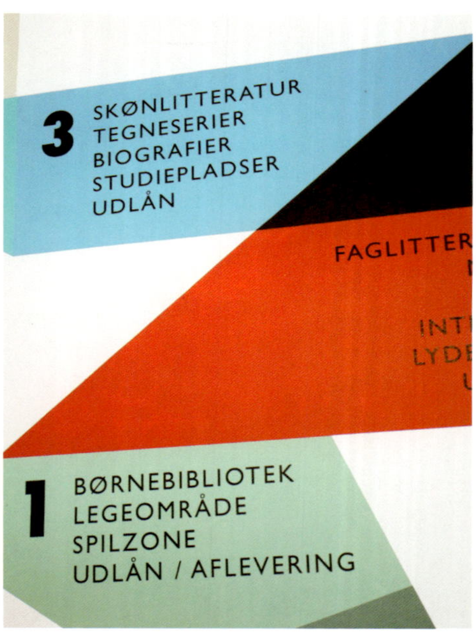

A large geometric shape near the entrance shows the general outline of this library. Parts of the shape are repeated on the entrance to each floor in different geometric shapes. The tangram-like signage graphics animate the plain walls and imbue the reading area with intelligence.

Design Firm: Rama Studio **Photographer:** Rama Studio **Client:** City of Copenhagen **Location:** Copenhagen, Denmark

3 SKØNLITTERATUR
TEGNESERIER
BIOGRAFIER
STUDIEPLADSER
UDLÅN
FAGLITTERATUR
MUSIK
FILM
INTERNET
LYDBØGER
UDLÅN 2
1 BØRNEBIBLIOTEK
LEGEOMRÅDE
SPILZONE
UDLÅN / AFLEVERING
1 BØRNEBIBLIOTEK
LEGEOMRÅDE
SPILZONE
UDLÅN / AFLEVERING
FAGLITTERATUR
MUSIK
FILM
INTERNET
LYDBØGER
UDLÅN 2
3 SKØNLITTERATUR
TEGNESERIER
BIOGRAFIER
UDLÅN

eventyrlige illustrationer
udstilling af Renata Fucikova

HOTEL & HOUSING

Wayfinding in Hotel & Housing: Making For a Better Stay

High quality hotels and resorts not only accommodate guests, but also provide them a homey experience and a sense of security. Therefore a signage system in these accommodations most importantly needs to be easily recognized, gently leading guests to their suites. Besides that, designers love to use warm, bright colors to invite guests to enjoy a rejuvenating stay. By catering to the specific themes and features of different hotels and apartments, the signage system also help to shape the brand persona.

Hotel 3K Europa

Design Firm: P-06 Atelier **Designer:** Nuno Gusmão, Mário Videira, Joana Proserpio **Photographer:** João Morgado **Client:** Grupo 3K **Location:** Lisbon, Portugal

CENTO E UM	DUZENTOS E UM	TREZENTOS E UM	QUATROCENTOS E UM	QUINHENTOS E UM	SEISCENTOS E UM	SETECENTOS E UM
101	201	301	401	501	601	701

To add European flair to the hotel, a signage project consisting of wall signs, chromatic design and thematic illustrations was developed. Specific color codes are designated to each floor to create a diversified atmosphere. Each floor applies from corresponding color code to interior elements such as stairways, door numbers and maps. Similarly, every room is embellished by cultural symbols from different European countries to establish a distinct identity. The signage size is flexible to meet individual needs. While it is intentionally oversized in the parking lot and main stairways, making the guidance apparent, the signage on the wall is simple and intuitive. The designer also integrated signage information into the graphics design and let the visual memory inform travelers which floor and room they are in. It caters to the European vision and makes the hotel a modern, international and open-minded getaway for tourists.

PISO -1 (1/100)

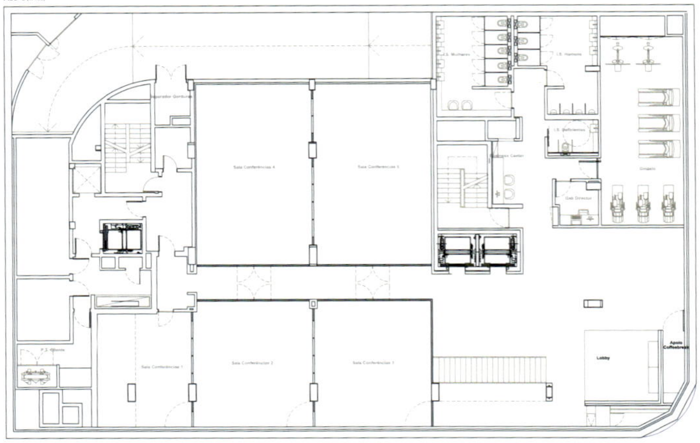

PISO 0 (1/100)

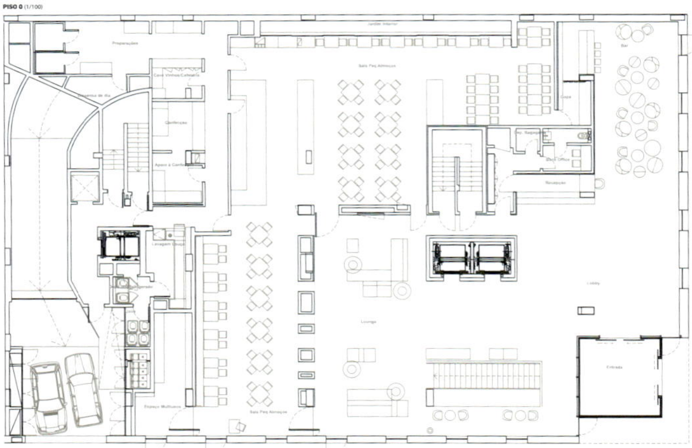

PISO 1 (1/100)

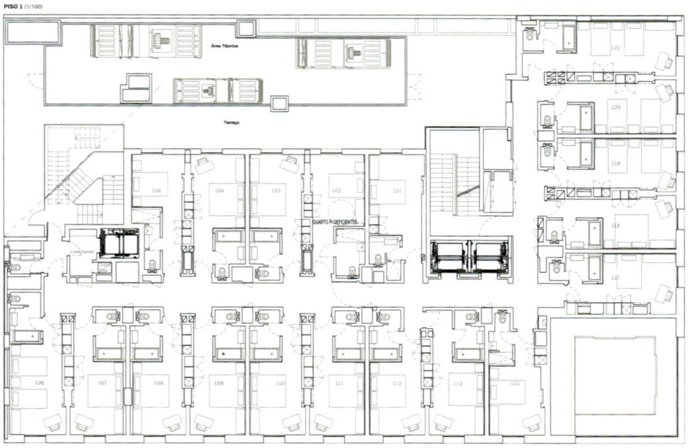

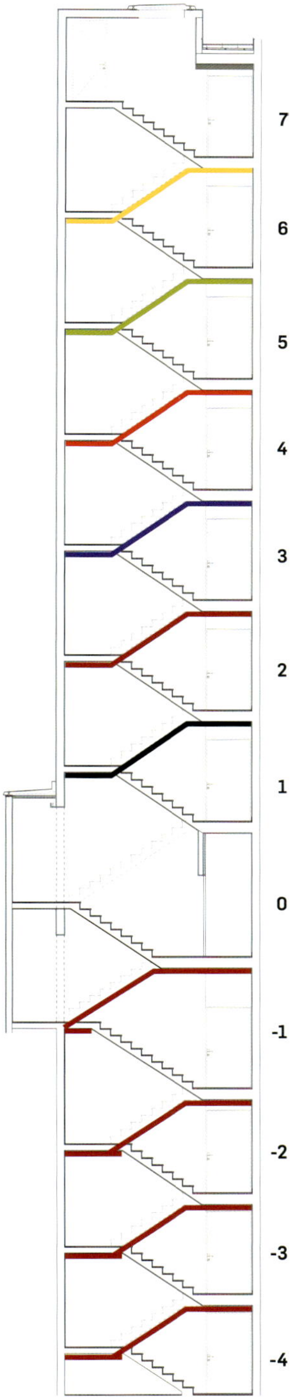
7
6
5
4
3
2
1
0
-1
-2
-3
-4

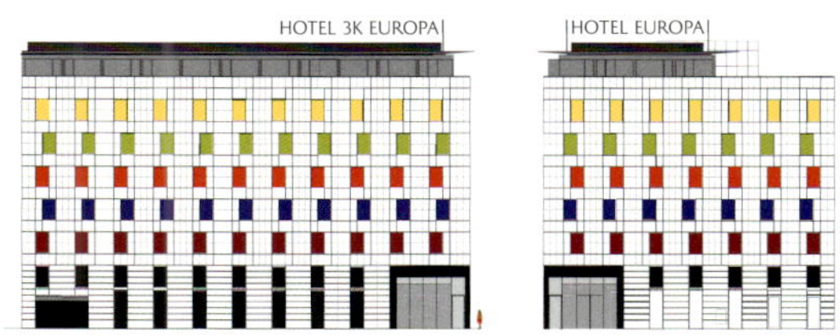
HOTEL 3K EUROPA
HOTEL EUROPA

HOTEL 3K EUROPA
HE

HOTEL 3K EUROPA
-3

Tobaco Hotel

Refurbished from an old factory building, the Tobaco Hotel has a bright and spacious interior. To further highlight its industrial background, the hotel's signage system employs vertical, back-illuminated panels mounted on the wall with black-lettered wayfinding information; the yellow directing lines on the floor reliably guide guests. With this shining and well-legible signage form, guests can easily locate facilities. Combined with the vivid color scheme, the signage system emphasizes the modern characteristics of the hotel.

Design Firm: EC-5 **Designer:** Luiza Jodłowska, Martyna Nowak, Hanna Pietras, Piotr Płóciennik **Photographer:** Michał Mazurowicz
Client: Arche Sp. Z o.o. **Location:** Łódź, Poland

HOTEL
TOBACO
HOTEL
TOBACO

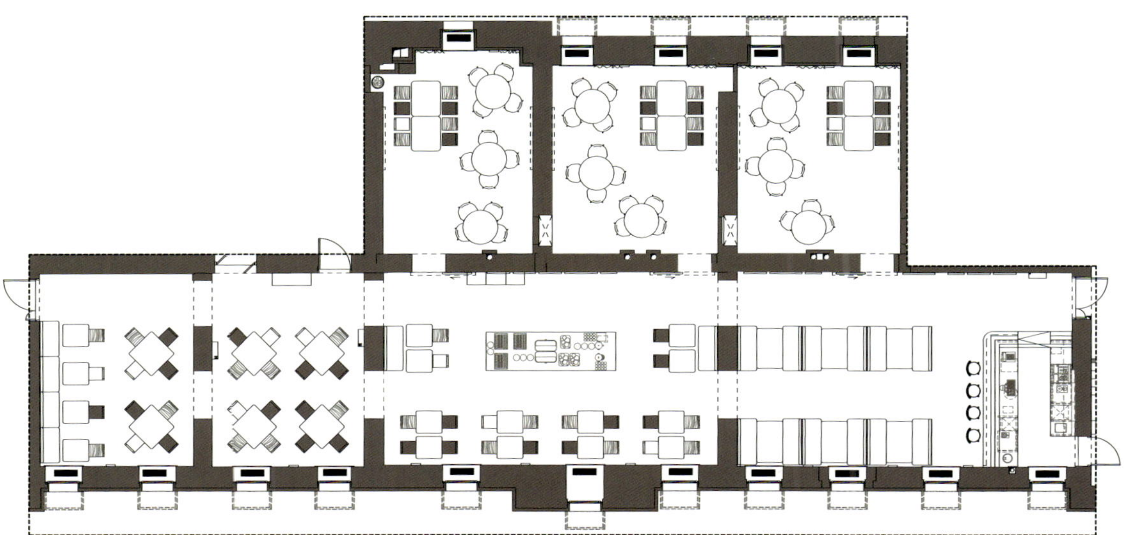

0
011-016
017-045
017

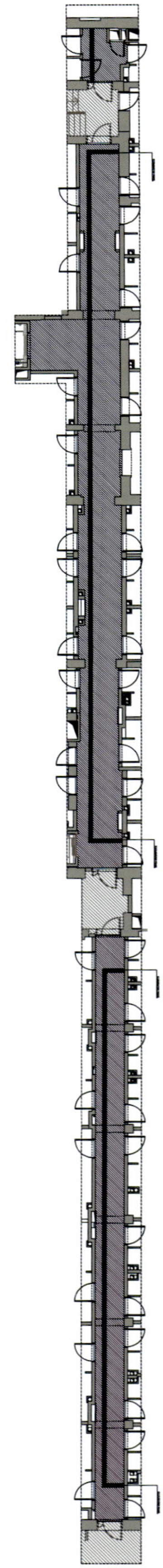

07
108
1
101-108
109-138

1
101-108
109-138

03

VEGA building

A new, Art Deco style, 40 apartment building, the name VEGA refers to the plane famously flown across the Atlantic. The artists developed designs that created an identity using the clean lines of Art Deco style as a contemporary influence. Building on the narrative, they developed a system that utilises the elegant form of the Vega plane and chose a font that is modern, legible and contemporary, and which complemented the building and the developing story.

Wanting a "light touch", the final design took a sensitive approach using accented colours for each floor and individually cut stainless steel signage lettering that was mounted directly onto building surfaces, respecting the architectural lines. Some fun elements are included using the plane's silhouette in the car park to mark parking spaces.

This clean and contemporary signage system innovatively decorates the industrial style apartment building, creating a cheerful atmosphere.

Design Firm: Yelo Wolf **Designer:** Richard Wolfstrome, Andy Parsons **Photographer:** Jim Stephenson **Client:** Southern Housing **Location:** Hove, England

BB15
BB16
BB17

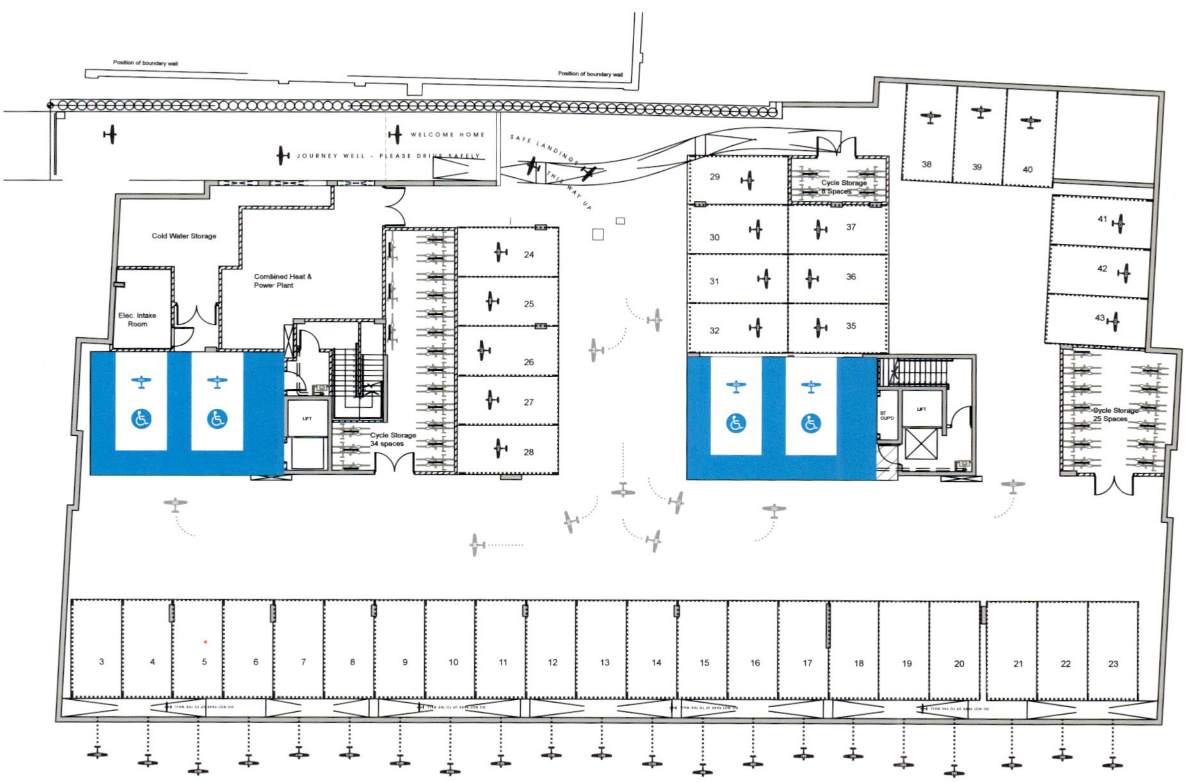
Position of boundary wall
Position of boundary wall
WELCOME HOME
JOURNEY WELL - PLEASE DRIVE SAFELY
SAFE LANDINGS
THIS WAY UP
Cold Water Storage
Combined Heat & Power Plant
Elec. Intake Room
LIFT
Cycle Storage 34 spaces
Cycle Storage 6 Spaces
Cycle Storage 25 Spaces

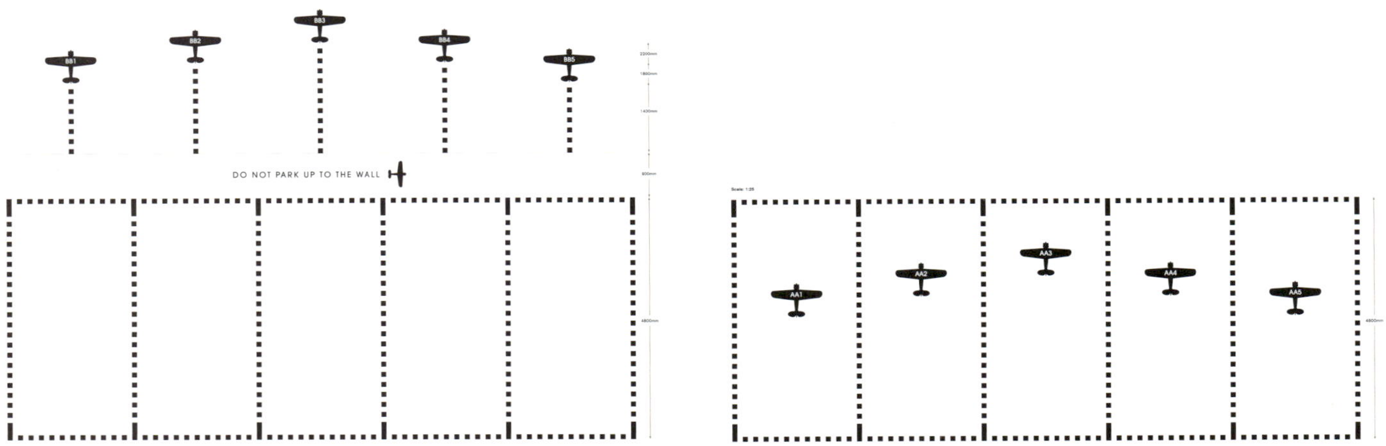
BB1
BB2
BB3
BB4
BB5
DO NOT PARK UP TO THE WALL
AA1
AA2
AA3
AA4
AA5

FLOOR APTS
3 35-40
2 29-34
1 23-28
G 17-22

Werkheim Uster

Werkheim Uster is an institution where disabled people live and work. The workshops here include wood, metal and silkscreen production.

The signage system uses the wooden materials produced there to assemble the names of residents and other wayfinding data on the wall. A typeface with as few angles as possible was created and applied throughout the signage project. In the invitingly colorful suroundings the signage clearly and amiably guides people while including tenants with mental disabilities into the production process.

Design Firm: Hi – Megi Zumstein & Claudio Barandun **Designer:** Megi Zumstein, Claudio Barandun, Fokusform, David Weisser **Photographer:** Openminds, Stefan Wülser **Client:** Werkheim Uster **Location:** Uster, Switzerland

1
WOHNUNGEN 3-6
SEEBLICK/EINBLICK
WC/GARDEROBEN
WERKSTÄTTEN

U1
SEEBLICK/EINBLICK
WC/GARDEROBEN

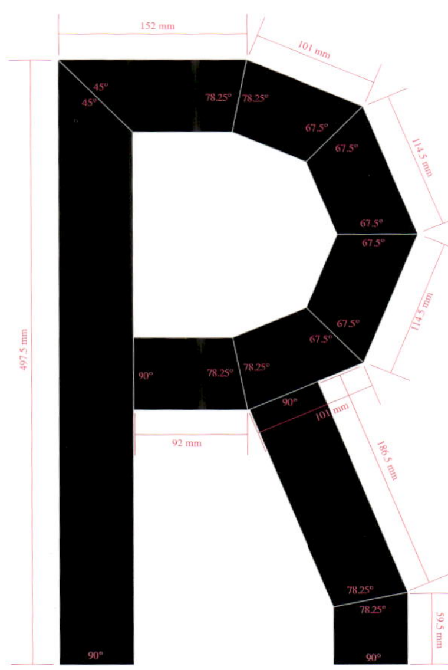
152 mm
101 mm
114.5 mm
114.5 mm
497.5 mm
92 mm
101 mm
186.5 mm
59.5 mm
45°
45°
78.25°
67.5°
90°

Zuri Express

The hotel's initial name "pelangi" which means "rainbow" had inspired its signage design. Colors derived from the rainbow respectively cover the lift lobbies of seven levels to distinguish and accentuate floor information. The wayfinding icons also utilize rainbow colors to assemble lively pictograms. The project builds brand visual identity into the signage system and interior design, making the hotel an animative and sweet place which warmly welcomes its guests.

Design Firm: Sciencewerk CIENCEWERK **Designer:** Sacharissa Kurniawan **Client:** Zuri Express Hotel Indonesia **Location:** Surabaya, Indonesia

203

STAY
SIMPLE,
SIMPLY
STAY

STAY
SIMPLE,
SIMPLY
STAY
HAVE
A
NICE
DAY :)

Hotel Minho

Design Firm: R2 **Designer:** Lizá Ramalho and Artur Rebelo, assisted by Artur Faria **Photographer:** Eva Sousa, Lizá Ramalho, Filipe Braga

Client: Hotel Minho **Location:** Vila Nova de Cerveira, Portugal

The designers were asked to create a new design concept for this hotel, which should reflect the modern nature of the building as well as the local characteristics. In order to achieve this, a straightforward and geometric typeface was composed. The symbol of the region - a stag - was also included in various positions: standing, walking and lying down. The pictograms utilize a lot of angles which are reminiscent of antlers. These elements appear throughout the design project. This signage design effectively presents the distinctive local features while adding a natural and elegant flavor to this hotel.

MGC Bistrica

To serve the main inhabitants of this senior-citizen resort, the signage system focuses on a graphical language that has been adjusted to their needs and utilizes fresh colors to release pleasant and positive emotions. The signs adopt round shapes to make them easy on the eyes, and also have easy recognition and interface usability. This wayfinding system has turned this resort into a colorful and cozy space.

Design Firm: Studio 360 **Designer:** Vladan Srdic **Photographer:** Studio 360 **Client:** IMP, d.d. **Location:** Domžale, Slovenia

1
A

KNJIŽNICA

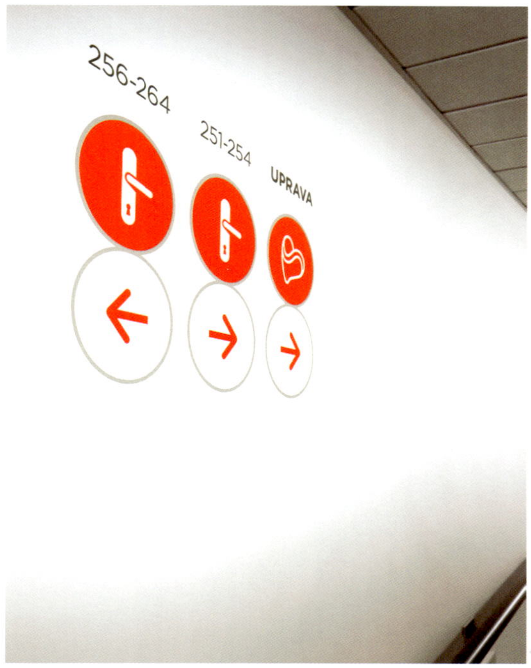
256-264
251-254
UPRAVA

RECEPCIJA
pritličje
UPRAVA
2
OS
2-6

DSO
1-3
GARAŽA
klet

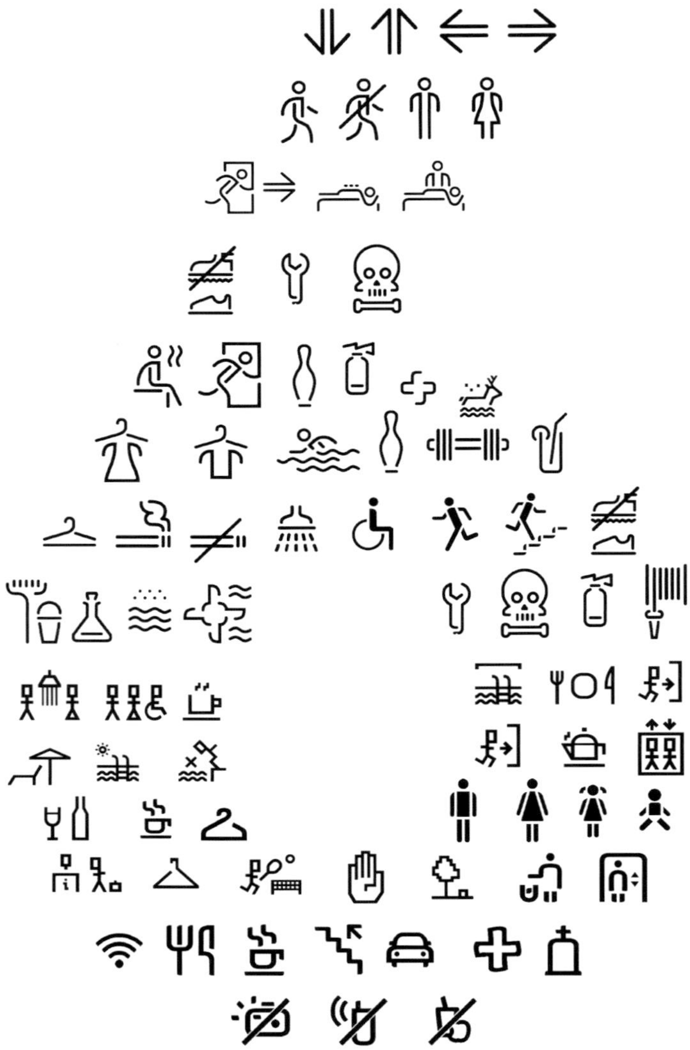

OUTDOORS

Wayfinding Outdoors
Spaces made smart

This kind of wayfinding system usually adopts the form of posts which deliver textual information and direction at the same time. The significance of a map is obvious in outdoor areas; it clearly informs visitors of the overall geographical layout. In designing an outdoor signage system, one crucial factor is that the wayfinding should be naturally integrated with the environment. Either by mounting it on natural materials such as stone and wood, or by expending historical and cultural elements, the signage system works in harmony with nature and urban surroundings. Using authentic local colors, the wayfinding attracts tourists and functions as a companion of its ecological and environmental background.

Wayfinding: 100 NYC Public Sculptures

This outdoor wayfinding project is made up of signage containing distances drawn from GPS coordinates between 100 public sculptures and a group of wooden posts at Socrates Sculpture Park, New York City. This wayfinding device is designed in the form of a wind vane, directing to the right location with small images of each sculpture on corresponding branches of the signpost. This signage work combines the longstanding practice of printmaking with the use of new technology: the GPS coordinates, a digital compass, and an online map where people can view for further information.

This site-specific project helps viewers explore without travel or motion, and proves how a journey within a specific geographic sphere can be a work of art in itself. Visitors participate in this project by experiencing each sculpture, whether through the original works or their representative illustrated counterparts, paying attention to the very specific, transformative gap between object and audience.

This signage system activates new definitions of original mapped sculptures. It transforms the definition of public art by introducing a more robust component of exploration and navigation, and engages the public to interpret the original work through their physical journeys, experiences, and memories. The established meanings of sculptures will change as they are discussed by people face-to-face on-site or online through social networks, bringing them to life through media. The signage work also contributes to the cultural image of NYC and promotes the city's identity.

Artist: Bundith Phunsombatlert **Photographer:** Bundith Phunsombatlert **Commissioned by:** Socrates Sculpture Park **Location:** New York, USA

2.95 mi

4.09 mi

3.95 mi

SOMETIMES
14.23 mi

2.41 mi

22 mi

2.41 mi

Ecovia e Ciclovias do Litoral Sudoeste

Bikeways require a simple, clear and readable signage system through the duration of the course. The designer redesigned graphics and colors in a contemporary style while preserving the same wayfinding elements, dimensions and shapes from the old system. When cars and bikes share the same track, the signage is basically the official standard traffic signs along with a bikepath identifier to simplify the system and avoid misunderstanding.

The wayfinding system effectively coveys information to cyclists. Aesthetic pictograms and bright yellow highlights visually integrate the signage with the diversity of landscapes along the way and give a new identity to the sign system.

Design Firm: P-06 Atelier **Designer:** Nuno Gusmão, Pedro Anjos **Photographer:** P-06 Atelier **Client:** Polis Litoral Sudoeste **Location:** Alentejo, Portugal

sistema composto por peças em betão moldado, com inscrições gravadas e pintadas

marco hectométrico
numeração sequencial
de 1 a 10

marco kilométrico
com indicação frontal do km, do troço e indicações laterais de orientação para os dois sentidos da via

marco miriamétrico
com indicação frontal de 10 em 10 km e indicações laterais de orientação para os dois sentidos da via

marco de info específica
com indicação frontal de informações, tipo cursos de água ou outros e indicações laterais de orientação para os dois sentidos da via

marco direccional
(antigo marco de extrema) indicação de direcção de percurso em casos de opções como cruzamentos, etc

Parc Riu Llobregat

Made from local tree varieties, the wooden signage block at the access pointing to the riverside park gives people overall wayfinding information. The kilometre markers serve as seats along the way to offer points of rest. The L-shaped metallic panel lends itself to information on both sides, with the narrow side being used for the map. The park logo is designed to visualize the river's courses passing along the park. This symbol includes a collection of specific pictograms. A mono-linear type face was chosen to reflect the routes and paths the park offers, and rounded shapes are used to convey a friendly, playful tone. The blue and brown colors represent the river and the land, respectively.

This signage system is both informative and practical, but not intrusive. With the wooden form and pictograms advocating for nature, it's assimilated in the landscape.

Design Firm: Clase bcn **Designer:** Clase bcn **Photographer:** Jordi Surroca **Client:** Àrea Metropolitana de Barcelona **Location:** Barcelona, Spain

Km 8
30
6
0

Sant Boi
parc riu llobregat

1
2
3
4
6
7
5
1 Masia de Can Comas
2 Parc lúdic fluvial
3 Espais naturals del Delta
4 Cal Tet i Ca l'Arana
5 Torre Mirador
6 Caserna dels Carrabiners
i Semàfor
7 Sistema de platges

Falls Creek Alpine Resort

In this ski resort, a modular signage system was created to provide a wide variety of directive information to suit the complicated village layout. The red-colored posts, or simply red posts lead to an eye-catching effect in the background of snow. The design of the sign system promotes the highest possible visibility while retaining a lithe supporting structure. It guides visitors through this natural region through the concept of environmental protection, contributing to a sustainable tourism experience.

Design Firm: Büro North **Designer:** Soren Luckins, Finn Butler, Ante Ljubas, Tom Allnutt, Dave Williamson **Photographer:** Daniel Colombo
Client: Falls Creek Alpine Resort **Location:** Victoria, Australia

Snowgum Lane

Village Map

Herdade do Esporão

Design Firm: White Studio **Designer:** Eduardo Aires **Photographer:** Alexandre Delmar **Client:** Herdade do Esporão **Location:** Alentejo, Portugal

Herdade do Esporão is a winery estate with a large farming plot. Its outdoor signage relies on big rocks found in the area; the wayfinding is printed on processed schist stones. These signage blocks were strategically placed to guide visitors through this agricultural area. By displaying wayfinding information on the existing stone blocks, the project works in harmony with manor's landscapes. The combination of modern typographic solutions and primitive, imposing geological elements integrates the signage system into nature.

La Molina

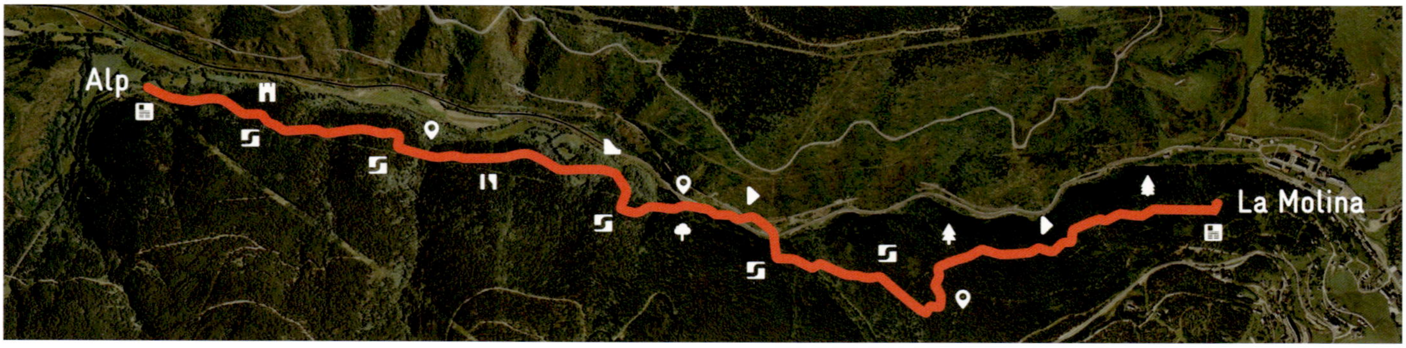

A signage project with rounded pictograms and bright colors was chosen for this mountain trail. The designer strategically positioned the wayfinding signs along this trail to offer information to hikers. As wooden signage boards naturally complement the landscape, this pure signage system was perfectly blended into the natural environment.

Designer: Adrià Gómez, Sergi Diaz, Jaume Juan **Photographer:** Jaume Juan **Client:** La Molina **Location:** Barcelona, Spain

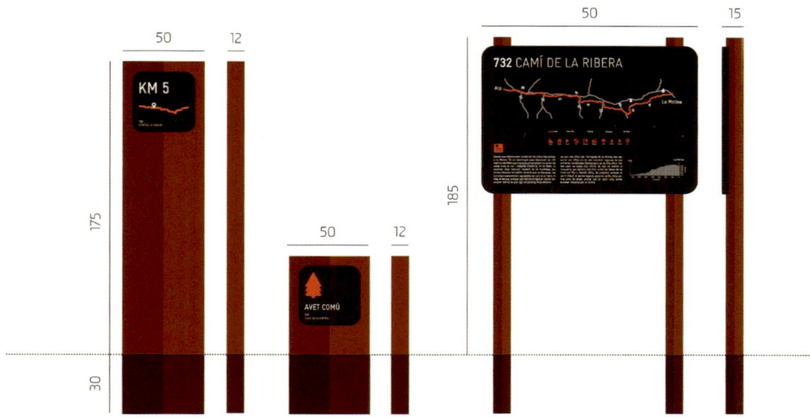
50
12
175
30
KM 5
50
12
AVET COMÚ
50
15
185
732 CAMÍ DE LA RIBERA
La Molina

DESNIVELL
PATRIMONI
TORRENT
LA MOLINA
INFORMACIÓ
KM 5
ESTRENYIMENT
ALP
PI ROIG
AVET BLANC
AVET COMÚ
MORFOLOGIA

KM 5

Makara Peak Mountain Bike Park

This wayfinding project of this mountain park aims to make navigation simple, increasing its accessibility for new riders. The large sign size allows the wayfinding material to be displayed clearly and legibly for riders at a great distance. The top right corners of sign boards have been cut off to draw attention to the arrow, subtly leading park users to the right direction.

The signage colors adhere to the internationally recognized grading system which indicates different track difficulties. The bright colors and information written on the boards inform people of the degrees of difficulty of their tracks. The text information is illuminated during the night so that a nocturnal walker won't be confused.

The track signs include a range of symbols serving two different user groups: the bikers and the walkers. In steeper, narrower tracks the wayfinding symbols for walkers are removed, implying that walking activities on these tracks are not safe. An online APP installed on mobile devices is invented to help users gather GPS data and easily find routes.

This signage system stands out from its surroundings without visually polluting the conservation park. By minimizing chaos and potential hazards, it also creates a safer outdoor environment for both mountain-biking and walking.

Designer: Oliver Ward, Josie Schultz, Rachael Jupp, Stephanie Tidey, Rhianna Field **Client:** Makara Peak Mountain Bike Park Supporters Group

Location: Wellington, New Zealand

Missing Link
Missing Link
To Summit
To Aratihi

Use Low Gears
!
End of trail
Snake Charmer
4WD Track
1.8 km

Koru
Missing Link
Trickle Falls
Snake Charmer
To Summit
To Aratihi

Missing Link
Intermediate
1.8 km
Two Way
To Summit
To Aratihi

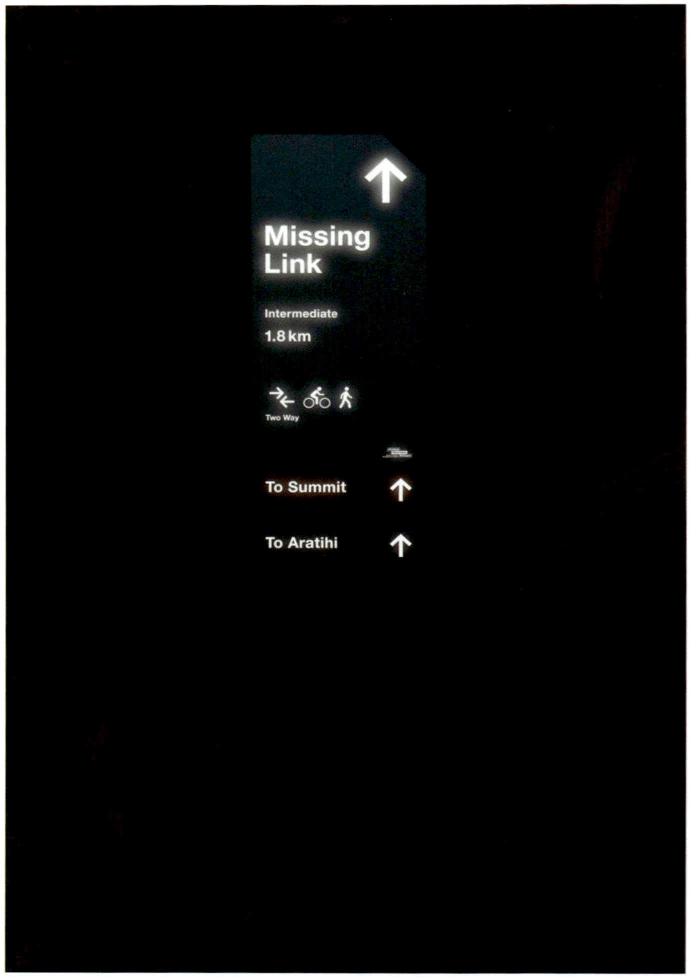
Missing Link
Intermediate
1.8 km
Two Way
To Summit
To Aratihi

Missing Link
Intermediate
1.8 km
Two Way
Track Signs

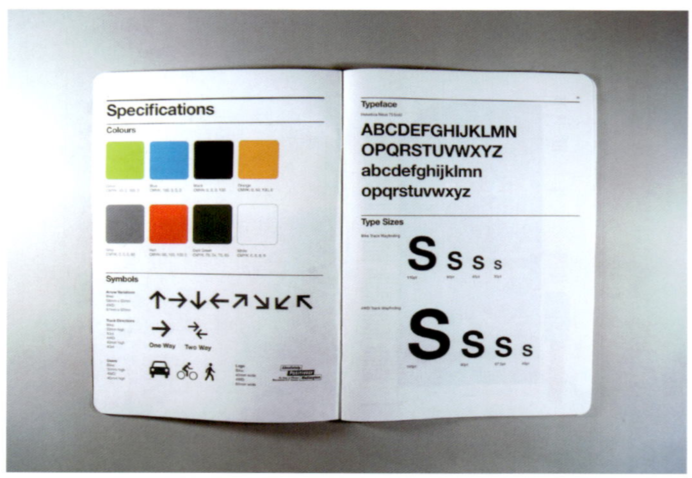
Specifications
Colours
Symbols
One Way
Two Way
Typeface
ABCDEFGHIJKLMN
OPQRSTUVWXYZ
abcdefghijklmn
opqrstuvwxyz
Type Sizes

VODA NZ 3G 4:20 PM
Bike Park
Route Finder

Route Finder
Find
Trending
Favourites
News
Select a level
Beginner
Easy
Intermediate
Advanced
Options
Estimated Time
2 hrs
Distance: 15 km
Origin
Destination
Generated Routes
Beginner 1
Start of your Route

The City of Metz

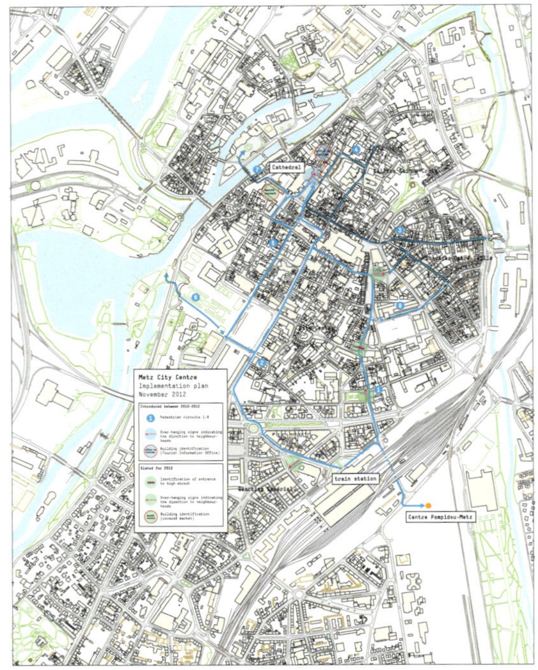

A novel wayfinding system was created for Metz city to respond to various issues which might arise, while visually presenting the city's historical culture.

Originating from the premise of messages written in space, the typography composition is laid out on horizontal lines that both link the letters and hold them up. The system can stand independently, adorn an existing feature or practically mark a building. The "Irma" font appears to thread over the stretched clear frames, without concealing the city's pre-existing architecture.

The signage in white is enhanced with touches of bright, even fluorescent tints; the posts in the streets are white, with colors fitting the environment painted on the edges and inside the lettering. By adopting materials cut by the water-jet from an aluminium block, there are no soldering marks or seams in the signs to mar the beautiful precision in the use of color within each letter and on the edges.

The signage identifying the entrances to covered markets resembles typographic canopies, with over-hanging messages demonstrating the diverse neighboring surroundings. This design casts enigmatic shadows of words on the façade and exhibits a profound cultural background of the city.

This poetic informational and directional signage system depicts the city as it is, subtly bringing information into context, revealing the urban culture and endeavoring to promote the city's image.

Design Firm: Intégral Ruedi Baur Paris **Designer:** Ruedi Baur, Eva Kubinyi, David Thoumazeau, Claudia Leuchs, Thibault Fourrier **Photographer:** Intégral Ruedi Baur
Client: Metz city council **Location:** Metz, France

MARCHÉ COUVERT
TOURTE LORRAINE, COCHON DE LAIT EN GELÉE,
PARIS-METZ,

CŒUR DE VILLE

ESPLANADE, ARSENAL
RUES COMMERÇANTES
OFFICE DU COMMERCE
SAINT-PIERRE-AUX-NONNAINS
PLAN D'EAU
PORT DE PLAISANCE
LAC AUX CYGNES
OPÉRA-THÉÂTRE
RUES COMMERÇANTES
LES ÎLES, TEMPLE NEUF
BASILIQUE SAINT-VINCENT

GRANDE CITÉ ROMAINE
CAPITALE DE L'AUSTRASIE
OFFICE
CAPITALE CULTURELLE À L'ÉPOQUE
CAROLINGIENNE VILLE LIBRE
DE
AU MOYEN ÂGE
CAPITALE DE LA PROVINCE
DES TROIS-ÉVÊCHÉS
CAPITALE DE LA LORRAINE
TOURISME
METZ A AUTANT D'HISTOIRES À
RACONTER QUE DE LIEUX À EXPLORER
CATHÉDRALE SAINT-ÉTIENNE
VITRAUX DE CHAGALL
MUSÉES DE LA COUR D'OR FRAC
LORRAINE CLOÎTRE DES RÉCOLLETS
MAISON RABELAIS PLACE SAINT
LOUIS OUTRE SEILLE COCTEAU
PORTE DES ALLEMANDS ARÈNES
PARC DE LA SEILLE CENTRE
POMPIDOU-METZ TRIANGLE
IMPÉRIAL ST PIERRE AUX NONNAINS
PORT DE PLAISANCE VERLAINE
BASILIQUE SAINT VINCENT
PLACE DE LA COMÉDIE

CŒUR DE VILLE
STADTKERN
CITY CENTRE
GARE SNCF
BAHNHOF
TRAIN STATION

ENTRE MOSELLE ET CATHÉDRALE,
AUX SOEURS DE SAINT-PIERRE-
DE RELIER LE PONT SAINT-GEORG
LES MOUVEMENTS DE TROUPE.
ELLE PRIS SON NOM EN 1761
ET DEVIENDRA GARTENSTRASSE
SOUS
L'ANNEXION.
RUE
DES JARDINS

MARCHE
COUVERT,
L'ARSENAL
OFFICE
DE TOURISME
PLACE
D'ARMES

Talk To

In reply to Turin's urban context, this micro signage system designed for pedestrians is composed of a customized set of pictograms and typeface that convey voices of Turin. This project uses three colors to distinguish three categories: orange for art and cultural sites, blue for public services and green for leisure facilities. The wayfinding information was created by the stencil and directly applied on the background by quick, versatile and unobtrusive means. This signage system guides pedestrians by accompanying them through the highlights of Turin while exerting a subtle influence on the city's image, promoting an energetic, bustling tourist city.

Designer: Marco Condello, Diego Federico, Gabriele Marchi, Antonio di Summa **Location:** Turin, Italy

Area gioco
Urban Barriera
Bagni pubblici

Moschea

520060
Museo Egizio
Super Mercato
Giardini Reali
Pronto Soccorso
Moschea
Bar

Stockwell Park

This housing estate has a wide variety of buildings that require an adaptable signage system. Using a sectional system of tiles combined with a customized pattern palette, the designers created a wayfinding project that delivers a balance of functionality and personality. The tile system allows the signage to adapt to a range of surfaces and configurations to fit varying surroundings.

The signs are clear and simple; they help first-time visitors as well as residents of the estate. The aesthetically pleasing graphics add a delightful flavor to the entire system, creating a more accessible and welcoming environment.

Design Firm: Hat-trick Design **Designer:** Jim Sutherland, Gareth Howat, Tim Donaldson, Laura Bowman **Photographer:** Phli Starling, Paul Grundy **Client:** Network Housing **Location:** England

CHUTE
HOUSE

Wynter
House

Stockwell
Road
Community
Centre
Norton
House

The City of Dandenong

The sign system which was put up in response to the public's request to understand the history of Dandenong complements the municipal revitalization program and boasts an inspiring urban landscape with a very strong design ethos.

The project introduced a delicate, ribbon-like structure which, although consistent in its basic form, is malleably able to assume various shapes in response to existing structures, furniture or landscapes. The signage structure is eroded at one end with laser-cut letter forms, creating a transparent quality, reducing the visual impact, and adding visual interest. The laser-cut words add a layer of meaning and elicit an emotive response. The remaining section of the structure forms a clean canvas on which to present detailed information. In its initial application, the structure exists in a folded, upright form, draped over a concrete plinth.

This robust wayfinding system makes an important contribution to the overall revitalization of Central Dandenong and influences the manner in which public spaces are understood and experienced by residents and visitors.

Designer: Mike Heine, Steve Jones, Anthea Lemmer, Annie Berkeling **Photographer:** Murray Case **Client:** City of Greater Dandenong **Location:** Dandenong, Australia

HALPIN WAY

SETTLERS SQUARE

SETTLERS SQUARE
PEACE
LAND
HOME

Kuan Zhai Alley

As a tourist attraction, Kuan Zhai Alley preserves and displays a group of historic buildings where celebrities and nobility used to gather for parties in ancient times. In order to revivify the joyous scenes, the signage system adopts the style of classical Chinese panes with imitation lantern light to create a soft, hazy atmosphere. The signage is well placed and effectively guides people around this ancient architecture zone.

This signage design connects with the elegant tone of the block and the antique background, catering to the historic theme in this sightseeing district.

Design Firm: Prismdesign **Designer:** ChangYang, KaiXiong, ShuangWu **Client:** The Cultural Tourism Assets Marketing Management Company
Location: Chengdu, China

KUAN ALLEY
ZHAI ALLEY
JING ALLEY

窄巷子
ZHAIXIANGZI ALLEY
CHENGDU
WELCOMES
YOU

P
室内停车场
COVERED PARKING

窄巷子
ZHAIXIANGZI ALLEY
往宽巷子

宽巷子
KUANXIANGZI ALLEY

P
室内停车场
COVERED PARKING

窄巷子
ZHAIXIANGZI ALLEY
窄巷子
ZHAIXIANGZI ALLEY

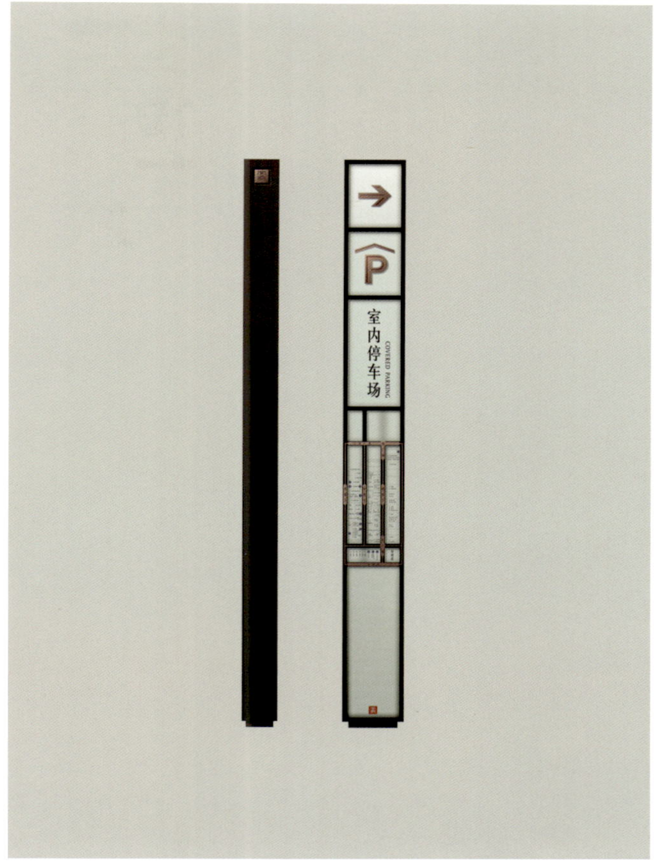
室内停车场
COVERED PARKING

室内停车场
COVERED PARKING
室内停车场
COVERED PARKING

卫生间
RESTROOMS
卫生间
RESTROOMS

INDEX

Luciana Mattiello and /STUDIOMDA team
www.studiomda.com.br
P72, P104, P172, P202

- M -

Mamastudio
www.mamastudio.pl
P198

Manic Design
www.wearemanic.com
P120

MALVI
www.mal-vi.com
P56

Marius Holtmon, Mette Landsem , Madeleine Skjelland Eriksen
mariusholtmon.com
P80

Marco Condello, Diego Federico, Gabriele Marchi, Antonio di Summa.
www.behance.net/n_o_u_m_e_n_o_n
P276

Massimo Acanfora
www.behance.net/MassimoAcanfora
P164

Masoud Alavi
studioalavi.com
P180

ma:design
www.madesign.it/
P46

Mikelis Putrams, Linda Krumina
www.made.lv
P42

Mohammad Hamed Zeinali
www.esadore.com
P210

- N -

Nivard Thoes
250g.nl
P212

Nosigner
nosigner.com
P144

- O -

Oliver Ward, Josie Schultz, Rachael Jupp, Stephanie Tidey, Rhianna Field
cargocollective.com/rachaeljupp
stephtideydesign.com
www.oliverward.co.nz
josieschultz.com
www.behance.net/rhianna-field
P268

- P -

P-06 Atelier
www.p-06-atelier.pt
P84, P192, P194, P234,P258

Prismdesign
www.prism-brand.com
P282

- R -

R2
www.r2design.pt
P20, P140, P250

Rama Studio
www.ramastudio.dk
P224, P228, P230

Richard Wise
www.into-corporate.com
P38

- S -

Sacharissa Kurniawan
sciencewerk.net
P248

Sid Lee
sidleearchitecture.com
P112

Space Agency
www.spaceagency-design.com
P108

- T -

The Box Brand Design Co., Ltd
www.boxbranddesign.com
P30

Tigran Kazaryan
www.mountteam.ru
P54

Tom Lloyd
www.abetteraande.com
P60

- U -

Un.titled
un.titled.co.uk
P214

- V -

Vladan Srdic
www.studio360.si
P118, P124, P252

- Y -

Yelo Wolf, Richard Wolfstrome, Andy Parsons
www.wolfstrome.com
P242

ACKNOWLEDGEMENTS

We would like to thank all the designers and contributers who have been involved in the production of this book. Their contribution is indispensable in the compilation of this book. We would also like to express our gratitude to all the producers for their invaluable opinions and assistance throughout this project. And to the many others whose names are not credited but have made specific input in this book, we thank you for your continuous support.